PATRICK KEILLER · ROB

TOPOGRAPHICS

Patrick Keiller

Robinson in Space

AND A CONVERSATION WITH PATRICK WRIGHT

REAKTION BOOKS
by arrangement with the BBC

Published by Reaktion Books Ltd
11 Rathbone Place, London W1P 1DE, UK

First published 1999

Printed and bound in Great Britain by
BAS Printers Limited, Over Wallop, Hampshire

British Library Cataloguing in Publication Data

Keiller, Patrick
   Robinson in space. – (Topographics)
   1. Cities and towns
   I. Title
   910
   ISBN 1 86189 028 1

The passage is from *Radical Subjectivity*, section 3 of chapter 23 of Raoul Vaneigem's *Traité de savoir-vivre à l'usage des jeunes générations*, written between 1963 and 1965, first published by Gallimard in 1967 and known in English as *The Revolution of Everyday Life*. This translation is from *Leaving the Twentieth Century*, translated and edited by Christopher Gray (London, 1974), in which chapter 23 appears as 'Self-Realisation, Communication and Participation'.

Sitting comfortably, I opened my copy of *The Revolution of Everyday Life*:

'Reality, as it evolves, sweeps me with it. I am struck by everything and, though not everything strikes me in the same way, I am always struck by the same basic contradiction: although I can always see how beautiful anything could be if only I could change it, in practically every case there is nothing I can really do. Everything is changed into something else in my imagination, then the dead weight of things changes it back into what it was in the first place. A bridge between imagination and reality must be built. . .'

In his 1985 essay 'The Geography of the Fifth Kondratieff', Peter Hall, now Professor of Planning at University College London but formerly of the University of Reading, wrote: 'Reading in England was a sleepy biscuit- and beer-making town until it was invaded by decentralised offices from London and high-technology factories from California.'

The following advertisement appeared in *The Times* on November 9th 1874: 'A Parisian (20) of high literary and linguistic attainments, excellent conversation, will be glad to accompany a Gentleman (Artist preferred) or a family wishing to travel to southern or eastern countries. Good references. A. R. No. 165, King's Road, Reading.' After Verlaine's death, Rimbaud's handwritten draft of this advertisement was discovered amongst his papers. ¶

Robinson's decision to move to Reading was reinforced by his hasty misreading of Michel de Certeau's *Practice of Everyday Life* (trans. Steven Rendall [Berkeley, 1984]): 'Reading frees itself from the soil that determines it' and '. . . reading is . . . a place constituted by a system of signs' (pp. 117, 176). Indeed, his entire project was inspired by this book: 'Every story is a travel story – a spatial practice' (p. 115). ¶¶

After Robinson published the results of his study of London, I didn't see him again for a long time, but I heard that he had been dismissed from his university position, and after a period in which he sank into a deep depression, had taken a part-time job teaching English in a language school in Reading, where he was now living.

He wrote to me in the spring of 1995, suggesting that I should come down to Reading on a visit. I was struck by the improvement in his mood and arranged to spend a few days with him.

Robinson met me at the station and took me immediately to King's Road, where he had identified the building which had been the 'coaching establishment' where Rimbaud was employed as a teacher of French in 1874. Robinson was very excited by this and the other literary associations of the town, which he praised with a euphoria reminiscent of that of Nietzsche for Turin, so much so that I was concerned for his well-being and the extent of his commitment to *the derangement of the senses*.

The *Maiwand Lion* commemorates the battle after which Dr John Watson was invalided *out of* the army and *into* his acquaintance with Sherlock Holmes.

Jane Austen was educated in two rooms above the Abbey gateway, which is next to the gaol where Oscar Wilde was imprisoned for the last years of his sentence:

'It is only shallow people who do not judge by appearances. The true mystery of the world is the visible, not the invisible . . .'

I did not think that Robinson's move to Reading was a good one. Despite his vision 'that other people could become fellows and neighbours', the fact is that, as Lefebvre says, 'The space which contains the realized preconditions of another life is the same one as prohibits what those preconditions make possible.'

The plaques on the *Maiwand Lion* include the following: 'THIS MONUMENT RECORDS THE NAMES AND COMMEMORATES THE VALOUR AND DEVOTION OF XI OFFICERS AND CCCXVIII NON COM OFFICERS AND MEN OF THE LXVI BERKSHIRE REGIMENT WHO GAVE THEIR LIVES FOR THEIR COUNTRY AT GIRISHK MAIWAND AND KANDAHAR AND DURING THE AFGHAN CAMPAIGN. MDCCCLXXIX – MDCCCLXXX' ¶

Jane Austen and her elder sister, Cassandra, were at the Abbey School during 1785–7. It occupied the rooms above the surviving gateway of the ruined abbey and was run by Mrs Latournelle, a French *émigrée*.

Oscar Wilde was moved to Reading Gaol from Wandsworth Prison in November 1895 because of poor health and served the remainder of his sentence there until he was released in 1897. Until July 1896, he was treated very harshly. Reading Gaol is now a remand centre for offenders aged 17–21.

The first quotation is from Lord Henry Wotton's monologue to Dorian on their first meeting at the beginning of *The Picture of Dorian Gray*. The Lefebvre quotation is from *The Production of Space*, trans. Donald Nicholson-Smith (Oxford, 1991), pp. 189–90. ¶¶

The Routemaster bus was designed for London Transport in 1953 by Douglas Scott (1913–1990). The Routemaster combined innovative engineering (monocoque construction, removable sub-frames, bolted assembly, air suspension, power steering) with a sociable interior lay-out, comfortable fittings and lighting, and the asymmetries of its half-cab front and open platform that recall the façade of a Georgian house. ¶

Nations for Sale, a study of Britain's overseas image, was produced in 1994 by Anneke Elwes for the international advertising network DDB Needham. Patrick Wright reported in the *Guardian* (December 31st 1994) that Elwes found Britain 'a dated concept', difficult 'to reconcile with reality', with a 'brand personality' entrenched in the past. ¶¶

Robinson had been living in a single room in a house in the northern suburbs. His job was poorly paid and insecure. He did not eat well, he seemed to know no-one in the town, and he had no telephone. His only reassurance was the presence of eighteen undeniably utopian Routemaster buses, operated by enthusiasts in a deregulated market. He could not keep up the effort of his euphoria nor hide his vulnerability, his fear of provincial England. He had been taunted by groups of homophobic youths when he ventured into the town in the evening.

He had once told me that he wished to become a spy, but was not sure who to approach. In the afternoon, he took me to the Chatham Street carpark, overlooking the Ramada Hotel, where it turned out he was now living.

He told me that some weeks before, he had received a letter from a representative of a well-known international advertising agency inviting him to a meeting at the hotel. These people had heard of his study of London and wished to commission him to undertake a peripatetic study of the *problem* of England. He had accepted this offer with alacrity and insisted that I join him as researcher.

British Invisibles – 'an
organisation which
promotes invisible exports,
in particular financial and
business services' –
produced a report, *Overseas
Earnings of the Music
Industry,* in 1995. This
claimed that the UK's
music industry had an
export surplus of £571
million in 1993. More
recently, it was estimated
at about £1 billion, whereas
in 1994 there was a trade
deficit in motor vehicles of
£6.8 billion.

On the other hand, the
total exports of the music
industry were £1.16 billion,
whereas the total exports of
motor vehicles were £9.4
billion, though the export
of value added is probably
much lower, given imports
of raw materials and
components and
repatriation of profit. There
is also the value of the
music industry to tourism.
Even so, it would seem
quite difficult to prove that
music actually *brings in*
more (in, say, wages) than
motor manufacturing, even
though imports of cars, etc.
greatly outnumber exports.

Adam Ant was briefly a
student in the Fine Art
department at Middlesex
Polytechnic, formerly
Hornsey College of Art. He
performed several songs in
the Reading branch of
HMV on April 7th 1995,
accompanying himself on
acoustic guitar.

Our first outing was to a record shop in Friar Street, where
Adam Ant was making a personal appearance. The music
industry is one of the UK's most successful and brings in
more money from abroad than motor manufacturing, its
products often characterized by sexual ambivalence and a
traditional English contempt for petit-bourgeois England.
Robinson had once taught at the art school where Adam Ant
was a student.

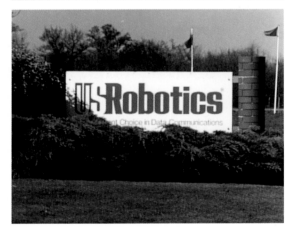

The next day, we visited the house at West Green built by General Henry 'Hangman' Hawley, who commanded the cavalry at Culloden – the former home of Alistair, Lord McAlpine, treasurer of the Conservative Party between 1975 and 1990.

The recent gate-posts and the obelisk are by the architect Quinlan Terry.

The obelisk bears an inscription in Latin: 'This monument was built with a large sum of money, which would have otherwise fallen, sooner or later, into the hands of the tax gatherers.'

'It is my belief, Watson,' said Holmes, 'founded upon my experience, that the lowest and vilest alleys in London do not present a more dreadful record of sin than does the smiling and beautiful countryside.'

The Winnersh Triangle business and distribution park is in the Wokingham constituency of John Redwood, admired by Gingrich Republicans in the United States as the leader of the 'revolutionary wing of Great Britain's Conservative Party'.

On Easter Monday, Greenpeace activists blocked the outfall from the Atomic Weapons Establishment at Aldermaston. Robinson had read that the growth of high-technology industry in the M4 corridor had been triggered by the number of government research establishments in the Reading area.

Henry 'Hangman' Hawley was born in about 1679 and was rumoured to have been an illegitimate child of the son of the Elector of Hanover, who later became George I. Hawley was favoured by George II and the Duke of Cumberland, and in 1745, aged sixty-six, he was appointed Commander in Chief in Scotland after the Jacobite victory at Prestonpans. At Falkirk, he was entertained to dinner by the wife of a Jacobite officer, so that when the Scots attacked he ran onto the field drunk and without his hat. The English were defeated with the loss of 600 dead and 700 taken prisoner. ¶

The Holmes quotation is from 'The Adventure of the Copper Beeches' in *The Adventures of Sherlock Holmes*.

The Greenpeace team shut off valves in a nineteen-kilometre double pipeline which carries the Atomic Weapons Establishment's effluent – believed to be contaminated with minute quantities of plutonium – into the Thames at Pangbourne Meadows. The valves are in a manhole next to the River Kennet east of Tyle Mill, not far from Aldermaston. The manhole was filled with six tons of quick-setting concrete and the cover welded shut. It took twelve days to unblock the pipeline and restore production.

War of the Worlds was first published as a serial in *Pearson's Magazine* in 1897. In chapter 2 of the book, the Martian projectile falls on Horsell Common 'not far from the sand-pits'.

Buckminsterfullerenes were proposed as a joke in 1966 by Dr David Jones of Newcastle University. In 1985, Professor (now Sir) Harry Kroto of Sussex University and Robert Curl and Richard Smalley of Rice University in Texas observed a previously unknown molecule of carbon in interstellar dust. They then found it in soot on Earth. The molecule consists of sixty atoms of carbon in a spherical geodesic arrangement and was named after the architect Richard Buckminster Fuller, who developed geodesic geometry as the structural concept of geodesic domes. The three co-discoverers shared the Nobel Prize for Chemistry in 1996.

In January 1996, the physicist and writer Paul Davies, Professor of Natural Philosophy at the University of Adelaide, was reported by Tim Radford in the *Guardian* to have said that '. . . even now an average of 500 tons of Mars was estimated to land on Earth each year'.

The Martian meteorites are fragments of rock thrown into space by collisions with asteroids or comets.

On the centenary of the Martian landing on Horsell Common, near Woking, which was so vividly described by H. G. Wells, Robinson took me to see the crater.

He told me that there are more than 100 patents in microelectronics, nanotechnology and other fields for uses of buckminsterfullerenes, the large, spherical carbon molecules discovered in cosmic dust by British and other scientists, but they are all held abroad.

The Martians destroyed most of Surrey. Five hundred tons of Mars are estimated to land on Earth each year.

On St George's Day, a group of campaigners occupied land at Wisley, near St George's Hill, the private estate developed in 1911 on former common land where the Diggers had set up camp in 1649.

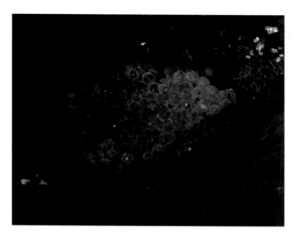

The group was 'The Land is Ours' and the spokesman was George Monbiot, writer and Fellow of Green College, Oxford. St George's Day is April 23rd. The site was 'set-aside' land beside the disused Wisley aerodrome. On Friday the 28th, the group processed to St George's Hill and performed a play, based on the legend of St George and the Dragon, on the practice range of the golf-course. This was featured on BBC2's *Newsnight*, together with a feature on golf, World No-Golf Day being a protest against the environmental destruction caused by the burgeoning demand for new golf-courses.

The Diggers settled on St George's Hill in April 1649. They were violently harassed and in August moved to nearby Cobham Heath, where they stayed until April 1650, when their huts were burnt down by vigilantes, and they dispersed. St George's Hill was enclosed in 1800 and bought by the Duke of York and, later, the Earl of Ellesmere. In 1911, a development company began building the present exclusive residential estate and golf-course. There is no public access to the hill.

In May 1996, 'The Land is Ours' occupied a cleared river-side site belonging to Guinness in Wandsworth, south-west London, and stayed there for several months.

The dishes' location is clearly marked on sheet 175 of the 1:50,000 Ordnance Survey map.

'We are challenging the government's whole philosophy about the pre-eminence of property rights,' said their spokesman, an Oxford University Fellow.

Robinson had not found any buckminsterfullerenes in the crater at Horsell Common, but he was impressed by the technology of the latter-day Levellers.

On the 28th, the eve of World No-Golf Day, they occupied the golf-course at St George's Hill.

May 4th was the day of the local elections. Despite the poor air quality, we set out for a walk in the bluebell woods towards Henley and came across a group of satellite dishes at a location we were asked not to name, which are the television receivers for the BBC's World Monitoring Service a few miles away at Caversham Park, established during World War Two.

With the coincidence of the Tory election defeats and the VE Day anniversary, there was a lot of talk about the 1945 election and about how laissez-faire had been kept off the political agenda until those who had participated in the war at decision-making level had departed from the scene.

Robinson says that unless Labour wins a *landslide* victory in a general election, there is always a Conservative majority in England.

Henley is the constituency of Michael Heseltine, who in 1995 was President of the Board of Trade. It was twinned with Boroma, Somalia, in 1981.

In the 1995 local elections on May 4th, the Conservatives lost over 1,700 seats and retained control of only twenty councils. The VE Day fiftieth-anniversary holiday was Monday, May 8th. The remark about laissez-faire is Denis Healey's.

At a very rough calculation, the Conservatives would have retained an overall majority of the seats in England if Labour had won with an overall majority of less than about sixteen. Labour needed an overall majority of about thirty-five seats to become the largest party in England, and an overall majority of about fifty seats to achieve a majority in England.

Even after the 1997 Labour landslide, most of the map of England is still coloured blue. Labour won most of the seats, but the Conservatives occupy more *space*.

The relationship between Henley and Boroma dates from the famine in 1979. Henley has sent generators and other aid to Boroma, and in 1996 there were some refugees from Mogadishu living in the town.

Defoe was born in about 1660. The *Tour* was written in various periods between 1722 and 1725 and published in three volumes in 1724–6. The thirteen journeys are probably based on a variety of experience – his travels as a merchant as far back as 1685, his work for Harley in the 1700s and some up-to-date research carried out specially for the book. It is later than most of the novels. In Letter 4 of the *Tour*, Defoe wrote that at the time of the Revolution of 1688, he 'went to Henley, where the Prince of Orange, with the second line of his army, entered that very afternoon'. In the introduction to the Penguin edition of the *Tour*, Pat Rogers wrote: 'He is visibly stronger on distribution and commerce than on industrial manufacture, perhaps because he himself had been in the wholesale business.'

John Hall-Stevenson, the 'notorious rake and libertine' who was a life-long friend of Laurence Sterne, was a member of the Hell-Fire Club. In *Tristram Shandy*, Eugenius ('a wise and cautious adviser') is based on Hall-Stevenson. Sterne was in the habit of visiting Hall-Stevenson's home, Skelton Castle ('Crazy Castle'), where as the 'Demoniacs' they imitated the antics of the 'monks' of Medmenham Abbey. This brought Sterne, a clergyman, into disrepute.

As we walked back to Reading, we passed the preparations for a celebration bonfire. Robinson told me that he had received instructions from our employer and that the next day we would begin the first of seven journeys which were to be the basis of our project.

This method had been suggested by his reading Daniel Defoe's *Tour through the Whole Island of Great Britain*, which is based on Defoe's travels as a *spy* for Robert Harley, the government minister in the reign of Queen Anne.

The narrative of Britain since Defoe's time is the result of a particularly *English* kind of capitalism.

With our contracts and expense account agreed, we set out to follow the Thames downstream to the sea.

Passing Fawley Court, a work of Sir Christopher Wren, and the nearby tunnels that allow toads to cross the road, we came to the Henley Management College and Research Centre at Greenlands, which offers degree and NVQ courses for individuals and corporate groups.

The village of Medmenham is near the abbey ruins where the Hell-Fire Club held their *Nocturnal Revels*.

20

MEDMENHAM

In 1817, the Shelleys moved to Albion House in Marlow, where she transcribed his *Revolt of Islam* and prepared *Frankenstein* for publication.

Marlow is also home to the UK headquarters of Volvo, Saab and Rank Xerox, and at Cookham, near the home of Stanley Spencer, is the headquarters of the Chartered Institute of Marketing.

The *Fountain of Love* at Cliveden was bought in Rome by William Waldorf, the first Lord Astor, in 1897.

It was at Cliveden that John Profumo first met Christine Keeler, who was staying at a cottage in the grounds. She was naked beside the swimming pool.

The Astors' pro-appeasement stance, and their entertaining of von Ribbentrop and Oswald Mosley, led to belief in the existence of the Cliveden Set, a conspiracy giving tacit support to Hitler's conquest of Europe.

Cliveden's prominence has always rested on its proximity to London, and its views. The present house is the work of Sir Charles Barry, the architect of the Palace of Westminster, and the view along the river was compared by Garibaldi with the mighty river prospects of South America.

Shelley sold the house in 1818, before leaving England for ever. He died in 1822.

Cliveden is unusual in that it is a large country house without a surrounding agricultural estate. The house and grounds have been owned by the National Trust since 1942, and the house has been let to Cliveden plc as a luxury hotel since 1985. Cliveden plc was floated on the stock exchange in 1996, and in July 1998 it looked as if it would be bought by Destination Europe, in which Bill Gates had a 10 per cent stake, following a takeover battle with a group headed by Goldman Sachs.

The *Fountain of Love* was designed and carved in Rome by the American expatriate sculptor Thomas Waldo Story (1855–1915), whose work was popular with wealthy British and American collectors.

At Maidenhead, we passed beneath Brunel's bridge of 1837, the longest-spanning brick-built arches in Europe and the scene of Turner's *Rain, Steam and Speed*.

In a letter from Ethiopia, Rimbaud imagined a son who would become 'a famous engineer, a man rich and powerful through science . . .'

With the departure of Douglas Hurd for the NatWest, there remained three old Etonians in a Cabinet of twenty-three, about an eighth.

Between 1868 and 1955, of the 294 Cabinet ministers who held office, over a quarter attended Eton, so that either Eton is no longer what it was, or, more likely, government is no longer an occupation that it's necessary for Etonians to be concerned with.

We left the river-bank at Windsor, where the 180-mile river-side path is blocked as it passes through the royal estate.

The river-bank was enclosed by Queen Victoria with an Act of Parliament in 1860, despite the prohibition of Magna Carta, which is displayed at the memorial at Runnymede erected by the American Bar Association in 1930.

Turner's *Rain, Steam and Speed – The Great Western Railway* was painted in 1843. If Rimbaud travelled to Reading by train in 1874, he would have crossed Brunel's bridge. He wrote to his mother on May 6th 1883: '. . . what is the use of all this indescribable suffering, if I'm not one day, after a few years, to rest in a place that I more or less like, and have a . . . son at least, whom I shall spend the rest of my life in training according to my own ideas, providing him with the best and most complete education which can be obtained today. . .'

On old Etonians, see W. D. Rubinstein, *Capitalism, Culture and Decline in Britain, 1750–1990* (London, 1993), p. 107. Until the changes following the 1995 Conservative leadership election, ex-Etonians in the Cabinet were Douglas Hurd, William Waldegrave, Viscount Cranborne and Jonathan Aitken. The new Cabinet was without Hurd and Aitken, but gained Douglas Hogg.

In 1997, Eton College revealed assets of £131 million, making it the UK's 600th largest 'company'.

The prohibition in Magna Carta had probably expired: 'All forests which have been made in our time shall forthwith be disafforested, so shall it be done with regard to river-banks which have been enclosed in our time.'

CROWN ESTATE
PRIVATE
GROUNDS

Nearing Heathrow airport, we came across a factory, the first we had seen since leaving Reading, all the more unusual since most toys today are made in China. Bendy products are made of natural rubber.

Heathrow airport, where the first commercial flight took off in 1946, is the busiest international airport in the world.

Robinson did not like to continue into London, fearing reprisals for his earlier study, so after a journey on the Underground and many hours wandering lost in tunnels, we emerged from the workings of the Jubilee Line extension, near the site subsequently chosen for the Millennium exhibition, and did not stop until we reached Beckton.

East Ham churchyard, opposite the Beckton ski-slope, is the largest churchyard in England.

The Heathrow Terminal Five inquiry began on 16th May 1995; in August 1998, it was still going on. The architects for Terminal Five are the Richard Rogers Partnership.

The Millennium Commission's choice was announced in February 1996; Greenwich was chosen in preference to Birmingham's National Exhibition Centre. The site on the Greenwich peninsula was derelict land contaminated by a former gas-works. The architects for the Millennium Dome are the Richard Rogers Partnership.

The disused gas-works at Beckton were the setting for the re-enactment of the fall of Saigon in Stanley Kubrick's *Full Metal Jacket* (1987).

See chapter 16 of *The Picture of Dorian Gray*.

Robinson was hoping to find some trace of the opium den frequented by Dorian Gray, by following the route described in the story, but he couldn't find anyone to ask . . .

'Coming soon on this site: a Warner Brothers 9-screen multiplex cinema, opening Easter 1996 . . .'

We had read that Ford were seeking government aid to build a new small car for Mazda, but that the Dagenham plant was facing competition from Valencia in Spain.

The development of Rainham Marshes was for the time being unlikely, as the Channel Tunnel rail-link terminal had been confirmed at Ebbsfleet, on the south side of the estuary.

Robinson thought he had discovered Dracula's house Carfax at Purfleet, until I pointed out that we were still in Rainham.

Ford have part-owned Mazda since the end of World War Two. Dagenham was chosen as the plant to build the Mazda, but apparently without subsidy.

In 1991, Michael Heseltine announced an initiative for private-sector regeneration of the east Thames corridor between Stratford and Sheerness which became known as the Thames Gateway. By 1995, a planning framework had been produced, but little else. Critics of the choice of site for the Millennium exhibition noted Heseltine's membership of the Millennium Commission. Ford's bid for a subsidy at Dagenham was also made in this context.

The house was actually Rainham Hall, owned by the National Trust.

When we *reached* Purfleet, he was surprised to find the view of London unchanged since he had left, despite both his predictions of imminent ruin *and* various attempts to link the Channel Tunnel with the regeneration of the estuary, balancing the pull of Heathrow in the west.

In *Dracula*, Jonathan Harker travels to Transylvania as an employee of the solicitor who is acting for the Count in his purchase of Carfax, an estate at Purfleet, which Jonathan describes in chapter 2: 'At Purfleet, on a by-road I came across just such a place as seemed to be required, and where was displayed a dilapidated notice that the place was for sale . . .'

The view upstream is from beside the Royal Hotel, now a popular Travel Inn.

In modern terms, individual British ports are not very large: Rotterdam – the world's biggest port – has annual traffic of about 300 million tonnes. The UK's total port traffic in 1994 was 538 million tonnes, greater than ever, but this was divided over a long coastline with a lot of ports. Generally, the increase in port activity has been much greater on the east coast than on the west, though this seems to be only partly as a result of EU membership and North Sea oil. Perhaps there was simply more scope for expansion. ¶

Robinson had purchased a copy of *Port Statistics*, a publication of the Government's Statistical Service, and every night he pored over it with a calculator, emerging from time to time with some new revelation: 'Port traffic continues to increase: exports have increased fivefold since 1965, most rapidly in the late '70s when North Sea oil was first exploited. Imports have fluctuated, but overall have risen by more than a fifth.'

The Port of London
Authority sold the Port of
Tilbury to its 830 employees,
who each received free
shares. These were worth
£23,000 when the company
was sold on to Forth Ports.
Over half the workers had
also bought shares, an
average £2,400 worth.
These would have been
sold for £51,000.

Defoe lived at Sleepers,
a farmhouse opposite
the church at Chadwell
St Mary, when he was
managing his part interest
in a tile works at West
Tilbury. His second
bankruptcy in 1706
followed the failure of this
business. The house is so
called because pilgrims
slept there before crossing
on the ferry at Tilbury.
Defoe is supposed to have
returned to the house to
escape charges of sedition
and to have written part of
Robinson Crusoe there.

The Thames estuary, from Teddington to Foulness, is
still the leading port in the UK, though in *foreign* traffic
the Humber ports outrank the total for London *and* the
Medway.

The Port of Tilbury, sold to its employees in 1992 for
£32 million, was bought recently by Forth Ports plc for
£132 million.

There is a house nearby where Daniel Defoe wrote part of
Robinson Crusoe . . .

Having spent the night at Tilbury, in the manner of the pilgrims, we spent the morning at the Lakeside shopping centre at Thurrock before crossing the river to Dartford. Robinson was anxious to see the town which is the birthplace of both Keith Richards and Mick Jagger of the Rolling Stones.

It was Environment Week in Dartford. We visited the landfill at Ebbsfleet, where Blue Circle were proposing to build a new town alongside the Channel Tunnel station, and Donald Trump is rumoured to be planning casinos.

Lakeside has 350 shops, more than any other UK shopping mall.

Dick Taylor, who founded the Pretty Things, was also from Dartford and played with Jagger and Richards in Little Boy Blue & The Blue Boys. Apparently, at one point in the 1980s, most of the senior A&R managers of the major UK record labels came from Dartford.

Ebbsfleet was once the site of Europe's largest cement works. Blue Circle was a client of Decision Makers, a lobbying company which employed Dame Angela Rumbold, then the Conservative Party's deputy chairperson, and which had sponsored Conservative fund-raising events in the Prime Minister's constituency.

The development, now known as Bluewater, includes 5,000 houses and a shopping centre only three kilometres from Lakeside with roughly 150,000 square metres in more than 300 shops, and a 'male crèche' designed to prevent heterosexual couples' shopping trips ending in rows. Twenty thousand more new houses are planned in the surrounding area.

By 1997, London and Continental Railways were proposing to build the Channel Tunnel fast rail link in two phases, with the first link from the Tunnel to Ebbsfleet and the more expensive completion to St Pancras postponed.

Marlow, the narrator of Conrad's *Heart of Darkness,* tells his story on a ship lying off Gravesend.

On the following evening, we reached the Isle of Sheppey.

'"And this also," said Marlow suddenly, "has been one of the dark places of the earth."'

During the Scott Inquiry, it emerged that in the 1980s Royal Ordnance, then owned by the Ministry of Defence, had shipped military explosives to Iran from Ridham Dock, a little-used quayside on the River Swale, between Sheppey and the Kent mainland. Similar small, out-of-the-way ports (where workers were not members of the National Dock Labour Scheme, abolished in 1989) were used to import coal during the 1984–5 miners' strike and featured more recently in coverage of the protests against live animal exports. See Tony Lane, 'Foreign Fuel, Foreign Ships and Disorganised Trade Unionism: An Alternative Interpretation of the Defeat of the Miners in 1984–5', *Work, Employment and Society*, x/1 (1996).

Knauf imports up to 300,000 tonnes of gypsum per year at Ridham, mostly from Germany, using its own jetty. The company has operated in Britain since 1988 and has another plant at Immingham. It is now one of the UK's largest suppliers of gypsum-based building materials.

In June 1996, the ILO called on the government to investigate Co-Steel's anti-union practices. Some employees said that they had been required to work more than seventy hours a week without overtime pay, and that 'dissatisfied' workers had been sacked.

Opposite Sheerness on the Isle of Grain is the automated container terminal of Thamesport to which ACL's ships were diverted for a period in 1996 during the Liverpool dock strike. In the Medway Ports brochure, Thamesport is described as the UK's most sophisticated container terminal, 'where driverless computerised cranes move boxes around a regimented stacking area with precision and speed'. Thamesport's managing director insists nonetheless: 'This is a people industry. The calibre and commitment of people are absolutely critical.' When Thamesport recruited its staff of 200, he said, 'I did not want anyone with experience of ports because this is not a port – it's an automated warehouse that just happens not to have a lid on it.' ⁋

The fully automated plant at Ridham produces 120 square metres of plasterboard per minute, the fastest-running production line in Europe.

Co-Steel Sheerness recycles scrap into steel rod and bar. The Canadian company evangelizes 'total team culture' in which overtime is unpaid and union members fear identification.

The Port of Sheerness, where 300 dockers lost massive share profits through being made redundant when they refused a pay cut, is now owned by the Mersey Dock and Harbour Company.

This was the end of our first journey.

The next day, we returned to Reading.

The pack-horse in the
picture is carrying brandy,
and the man is armed.

Didcot A is a 2,000-
megawatt coal-fired power
station which began
operating in 1970. Didcot B
is a new 1,400-megawatt
gas-fired power station,
part of the 'dash-for-gas'
which followed
privatization of the
electricity industry and
reduced the market for the
UK's deep-mined coal. On
the evening of January 25th
1996, electricity demand in
England and Wales peaked
at 48,800 megawatts when
several gas-fired power
stations were closed by gas
shortages, and power cuts
were only narrowly averted
for the third time in six
months. The incoming
Labour government placed
a moratorium on new
gas-fired power stations
in 1997.

Two weeks later, we set off again by the pack-horse road over
the hills towards Oxford.

The Oratory is an independent, selective secondary school
for boys. We were pleased to have an opportunity to study
the authorship of appearances in the English countryside.

As we began our descent, we could see the power station at
Didcot, which generates about 5 per cent of peak demand
in England.

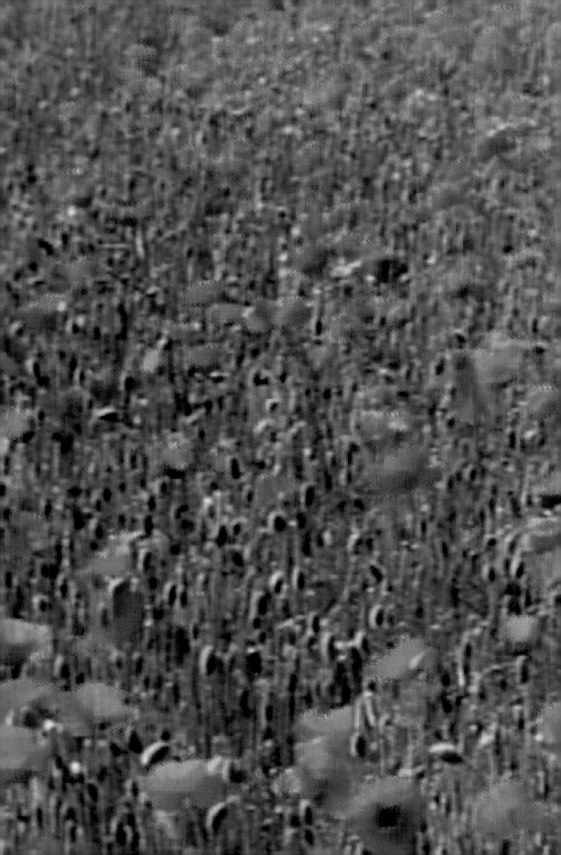

Nash first saw the Wittenham Clumps in 1907 and began to draw them in 1912. They appear in *Sunflower and Sun* (1942), *Landscape of the Summer Solstice* (1943) and *Landscape of the Vernal Equinox* (1944). In poor health, he worked with binoculars in a garden at Boar's Hill near Oxford, eleven kilometres away.

King Charles occupied Oxford after the battle of Edgehill in 1642. The university supported the King, but the city was more sympathetic to Parliament. The King set up his court at Christ Church.

Oxford was virtually unscathed during World War Two despite being a major centre for aircraft repair. In his book *Oxfordshire at War* (Stroud, 1994), Malcolm Graham refers to speculation that this was because Hitler had selected Blenheim Palace as his seat of government and Oxford as an administrative centre. The Royal Pavilion in Brighton, New Court at St John's College, Cambridge, and even Whiteley's department store in Queensway, London, are also supposed to have been chosen by Hitler for official use.

Near the river, we came across a break in the hedge where an excavation crossed the road.

From Wittenham Clumps, we could see that it led to Didcot, a gas pipeline to supply a new power station being built next to the existing one, which runs on coal. Didcot is operated by National Power.

The Wittenham Clumps were the *magic landscape* of the painter Paul Nash, but we had to press on, following the Thames upstream deeper into the interior of the country.

On the evening of June 12th, we arrived in Oxford, the King's headquarters in the Civil War, and Hitler's preferred capital had he occupied England.

In 1995, the surviving part of the Cowley works was making the Rover 600 and 800 models, based on Honda's Accord and Legend. In November 1997, BMW announced that it was to invest £300 million in a replacement for these models, in addition to £200 million already committed to Cowley for a new paint shop and a vehicle preparation and distribution centre.

In 1992, British Aerospace, who had bought Rover from the government for £150 million in 1988, were in financial crisis. A management buy-out was proposed for Rover which would have kept the company in British ownership and preserved the collaboration with Honda, but this failed because City banks would not lend the necessary £1.5 billion. Both BMW and Mercedes-Benz lacked expertise in small cars, front-wheel drive and four-wheel drive, and Rover offered the technology of the descendants of the Mini and the Range Rover. While BAe were still negotiating with Honda, who were unwilling to buy Rover outright, BMW made an unconditional offer which was accepted amidst criticism of BAe for alienating Japanese investment and suspicion of BMW's motives. Meanwhile, Bernd Pischetsrieder talked about reviving 'classic' British names like Riley and MG. ¶

Most of what was once the Morris motor works at Cowley was demolished in 1993, and the site is now a business park owned by British Aerospace, who sold the Rover group to BMW in 1994.

There has been little made of the fact that Bernd Pischetsrieder, the chairman of BMW, is the great-nephew of the late Alec Issigonis, whose innovative designs for Morris and its successors could probably have given the company a ten-year lead over Volkswagen in the European mass market.

At Magdalen (pronounced Maudlin) College, we visited the rooms once occupied by Oscar Wilde, who apparently enjoyed Oxford, though its atmosphere of stifled sexuality must have been even more striking then than it is today. The Fellows were not allowed to marry until 1877, and despite – or perhaps because of – the small numbers of women, open homoeroticism is still most unusual.

The President showed us the new buildings, by Demetri Porphyrios, which he described as examples of 'the architecture of the future'.

Our employer had suggested that we should buy a car.

According to Richard Ellmann's biography, Wilde seems to have spent much of his time at Magdalen worrying about whether or not to become a Roman Catholic. He did become a Freemason and worked on Ruskin's road-building project.

Porphyrios's design was selected from twelve entries in an invited competition for residential buildings and a small auditorium. A design by Ian Ritchie came second. The design adopts elements of what Porphyrios calls the Magdalen vernacular, though there are classical and other historical allusions. The buildings are of reinforced concrete and concrete block, faced with Ketton stone. The Prince of Wales visited the site in January 1995 to witness the burial of a 'time capsule' within the building. If one can stomach the fancy dress, the external spaces of this development are not unsuccessful, but for the visiting film-maker the interiors were banal, the quality and quantity of oak that had been lavished upon them suggesting only that the apparent modesty of architectural intent masked the usual collegiate vulgarity. Heating is by 'electric panels', and most of the rooms have open fires. A large balcony is inaccessible. The windows have leaded lights.

The car was actually a Riley Kestrel, a leather-and-walnut version of the 1100 series that was built at the former MG factory at Abingdon.

The locally produced Rover 800 was the first of ex-British Leyland's Honda-based cars to appear with a radiator grille based on that of the cars produced by the original pre-merger Rover company. By 1995, the entire model range carried them. The car appeared just after the 1992 general election, and for months one hardly ever saw them except in Whitehall. This, with a general greyness, the anthropomorphic novelty of the grille and the fact that some versions of the car were called *Sterling* made it somehow commemorative of John Major. The Rover 600 was launched in 1994.

The church of St Thomas the Martyr is in Becket Street, next to the former Royal Mail sorting office, near the railway station. In 1998, the sorting office moved to a new building in the business park on the former motor-works site.

While I was impressed by the favourable reports of the current local products, Robinson preferred the old 1100 we had seen earlier. I was sent to make the purchase, and he went off to the Bodleian.

We visited Christ Church, where, as librarian, Robert Burton lived a 'silent, sedentary, solitary, private life'.

The Anatomy of Melancholy appeared in 1621, under the pseudonym 'Democritus Junior'.

'The Jacobean melancholy, like our own,' said Robinson, 'was the result of a disorientation: you and I are deeply disillusioned people . . .'

Burton was vicar of St Thomas the Martyr between 1616 and his death in 1639. The porch is his addition.

I think we were never so happy as on the day of our pilgrimage to the memorials of Robert Burton.

The car was fitted with a radio. It turned out that it had belonged to a member of a successful Oxford pop-group.

Opposite the airport is Campsfield House, the privately run detention centre where up to 200 asylum seekers are held in prison-like conditions. In April, the inexperience of its management and staff had been severely criticized by the Chief Inspector of Prisons.

Campsfield House is run by Group 4 Security.

In 1995, Supergrass had a big summer hit, 'Alright'. The car did not belong to any of them, though in 1997 Mickey Quinn, the bass player, had a 1973 Triumph 2000.

Campsfield was the first private immigration detention centre. Group 4's fifty-nine 'detention orderlies' were recruited on the same basis as security guards and paid £4 an hour. A third were ex-army. The average stay of detainees was ten weeks, with 10 per cent being held longer than six months.

Comments by Judge Stephen Tumim followed a riot in June 1994 and included sixty-five recommendations for improvement. There was another riot in August 1997, after which non-participants wrote that they had insufficient food and were shut up in their rooms like prisoners and of immature officers who were always swearing and shouting.

'Whatever is fitted in any sort to excite the ideas of pain, and danger, that is to say, whatever is in any sort terrible,' says Burke, 'is a source of the *sublime.*'

We had arranged to visit the new Aston Martin works at Bloxham.

The literary stereotype of the sadistic Englishman endures in the drug excesses of contemporary aristocrats and as James Bond. Robinson had never paid much attention to James Bond, but he wondered if we shouldn't have bought a faster car.

The quotation is from part one, section VII of Burke's *Philosophical Enquiry into the Origin of our Ideas of the Sublime and Beautiful* (1757). The high esteem in which Margaret Thatcher and her colleagues held Burke leads one to wonder how much the Thatcher project's pursuit of policies which brought misery to millions was simply a matter of taste, or indeed of sexuality. ¶

In 1964, in *Goldfinger*, James Bond's car was an Aston Martin DB5. In 1994, it was suggested that the DB7, which was launched that September and seemed to promise a return to the company's success in the '60s, would appear in *GoldenEye*, the next Bond film. In the end, BMW offered a car, money and marketing support, so Bond drove a BMW. The small factory at Bloxham which produces the Aston Martin DB7 was built by Jaguar to produce the limited run of 350 £400,000 XJ220 cars. Jaguar and Aston Martin are both owned by Ford. Bloxham is in 'motor-sport valley', a crescent-shaped area centred on Silverstone in which much of the UK's motor-sport industry is concentrated.

67

The Temple family acquired the Stowe estate in 1593. They supported Parliament in the Civil War and were Whigs during the eighteenth century. Richard Temple (1675–1749) developed the gardens to bolster his political influence. The Temple of British Worthies (*c.* 1734), one of many in the gardens, is a pantheon of Whig heroes: Pope, Thomas Gresham (the banker), Inigo Jones, Milton, Shakespeare, Locke, Newton, Francis Bacon, King Alfred, Edward Prince of Wales (the 'Black Prince'), Elizabeth I, William III, Sir Walter Raleigh, Sir Francis Drake, John Hampden and Sir John Barnard, an obscure MP who supported Temple in voting against Walpole's excise bill. The Temple family motto was *Templa quam dilecta* – 'How delightful are your temples.' Stowe is about five kilometres from Silverstone, and when the track is in use the noise at Stowe is quite loud.

The quoted passage is from volume III, chapter 18 of *Tristram Shandy*.

We passed the United States Air Force's 603rd communications squadron, at RAF Croughton, and the Defence Clothing and Textile Agency, at Bicester. In the afternoon, we came to Stowe, described by the National Trust as 'Britain's largest work of art'. The house has been a public school since 1923.

In the landscaped gardens, based on Milton's description in *Paradise Lost*, is Kent's Temple of British Worthies, where we paid our respects to Milton for *Pandaemonium*; to Shakespeare for Yorick; and to Locke for *duration and its simple modes*, and *the succession of ideas*: 'For whilst we receive successively ideas in our minds, we know that we do exist, and so we estimate the existence, or the continuation of the existence of ourselves . . .'

At Bletchley Park, Alan Turing built the machine which cracked the Enigma naval codes in 1942.

On June 16th, we arrived in Milton Keynes, visiting the multi-denominational Cathedral in Silbury Boulevard opposite the shopping centre.

We stayed in Milton Keynes for a fortnight, leaving on July 2nd. We couldn't find the site where the Wiccans worship, which we had read about, but there is a Holy Well at Stevington which is easy to find.

To remain capable of waging war, the UK needed imports of 30 million tons per year. Turing arrived at Bletchley Park on September 4th 1939, the day after war was declared. In early 1940, he was put in charge of work on the Enigma naval signals, which was carried out in Hut 8. Turing developed the Bombe from earlier proposals by Polish cryptanalysts, and the first machine was put into operation in May 1940. By mid-1941, Hut 8 was producing a clear picture of U-boat movements that dramatically reduced losses of north Atlantic supply ships on which the war effort depended. In February 1942, a new Enigma system was introduced, and analysis had to begin again, with the flow of U-boat information finally restored in December. See Andrew Hodges, *Alan Turing: The Enigma* (London, 1983).

The Wiccans site is near Elfield Park, to the north of the bridge which carries road H8 over the main A5 through-road, from which it is visible. The Wiccans' application for a licence to use the site was opposed by fundamentalist Christians.The Holy Well is near the east end of the church. See Janet and Colin Bord, *Sacred Waters* (London, 1986).

A report entitled *Competing with the Best*, in March 1995, put the average cost of a night in a 1–2 star hotel in the UK at £53, 41 per cent more than the average of ten Western European countries. The British Tourist Authority's 1995 annual report and the 1997 *Which? Hotel Guide* both drew attention to the generality of overpriced, poor-quality hotels. The 'problem' of hotels seems to be worse in non-touristic areas.

The landfill site is beside the A421, near Brogborough, and is operated by Shanks McEwan. It has an eleven-megawatt power station which converts methane from the landfill into electricity.

Landfill in Bedfordshire is apparently the cheapest in the country, at £8 per tonne (in 1995). There is much more industrial, commercial and construction waste than domestic refuse. The contaminated soil from the Millennium exhibition site at Greenwich was taken to a landfill in Bedfordshire.

That night we slept in a shed. It was never easy to find a decent place to stay, but we generally took what was offered, imagining that the *problem* of hotels in England would be of interest to our employer.

We woke up outside what we thought must be the biggest, and *is* apparently the busiest, landfill in the country, one of several sites which had previously been exploited by the London Brick Company.

The next day's pilgrimages were to the airship hangars at Cardington, and to Bedford.

At a garage near St Neots, as we were thinking of trading in the 1100 for an old Volvo full of second-hand books, we heard on the radio that John Major had been re-elected leader of the Tory party.

Cardington was the centre of the UK's airship industry in the 1920s and '30s. No. 1 hangar was built in 1916 and enlarged in the late 1920s to house the 236-metre-long R101. No. 2 hangar was originally built for the Royal Naval Air Station at Pulham St Mary in Norfolk, and was moved to its present site and enlarged for the R100 in 1928. The crash of the R101 in 1930 led to the abandonment of the British airship programme. In 1995, No. 2 hangar contained the Building Research Establishment's test facility, with an eight-storey office framework, a mock-up hospital ward and a complete Boeing fuselage.

John Bunyan wrote *The Pilgrim's Progress* in Bedford. He was imprisoned there from 1660 to 1672 for preaching without a licence, and was minister of the meeting-house in Mill Street from 1671 until his death in 1688. The relief is of the pilgrim Christian fighting with the *foul fiend* Apollyon, on the plinth of Bunyan's statue at the corner of St Peter's Street and the Broadway.

St Neots is in John Major's constituency, Huntingdon. He announced the Cones Hotline in his party conference speech in 1992. As he was being re-elected as party leader, a maintenance gang began collecting traffic cones from the roadworks in the background of the picture.

Cowling is said to have considered that the New Right in Britain was the work of about fifty people, perhaps twenty of whom had Peterhouse connections. In the introduction to his book *The Impact of Hitler: British Politics and British Policy, 1933–1940* (Cambridge, 1975), he wrote that his analysis 'demands the assumption that it was neither morally obligatory nor prudentially self-evident that Hitler should be obstructed in eastern Europe'. In 1989, in an article entitled 'Why we should not have gone to war' in the *Sunday Telegraph* (August 20th), he added: 'It is wrong to assume that a dominant Germany would have been more intolerable to Britain than the Soviet Union was to become, or that British politicians had a duty to risk British lives to prevent Hitler behaving intolerably against Germans and others . . . Though the balance is a fine one, Russian (and American) domination of Europe after a long war, the destruction of Germany and the emasculation of the British Empire were probably worse for Britain than German domination of Europe might have been if that had been effected without war or the emasculation of the Empire . . . In matters like this, dogmatism is demeaning. It is equally demeaning, in the decade of Thatcherite realism, to present defeat as victory long after it has become clear that it was defeat.'

That evening, we reached Cambridge, which we *had* thought might be more congenial than Oxford. Our employer had been unable to secure us an invitation to dine at Peterhouse, the oldest and *nastiest* college, so we could not confirm its reputation for orgiastic revelry or gauge any lingering influence of Maurice Cowling, the unusually right-wing historian who was Michael Portillo's tutor.

The architects of the library at Jesus College were Evans and Shalev, with structural engineers Anthony Hunt Associates and building services engineers Max Fordham and Partners.

In 1995, Robinson College fell from twenty-third to twenty-fourth in a league table of finals results of the twenty-four Cambridge colleges, but the standard of bar-room sports was reported to be very high.

The A14 opened in 1994 and connects Felixstowe to the M1/M6 junction near Rugby. The section between Newmarket and Felixstowe was previously part of the A45.

In the morning, we had a look at Jesus College, where Laurence Sterne was an undergraduate and where the patrons of *architecture of the future* were, in our opinion, at least *better advised* than those in Oxford.

After lunch, and several games of table football, we drove off towards Felixstowe.

The Devil's Dyke marks the boundary of Cambridgeshire and Suffolk, soon after which we joined the newly renamed A14 trunk road (European route E28), which has cut journey times to the port.

78

See Defoe's *Tour*, Letter 1. A plaque records Defoe's stay in Bury St Edmunds in 1704, at the Cupola House, now an inn. Celia Fiennes had visited in 1698.

Despite having the largest foreign, non-oil traffic of all the UK's ports, the Port of Felixstowe does not cover a very large area. The larger of its two container terminals handles over a million containers per year, but achieves this with only five berths for the largest container vessels. In Letter 5 of the *Tour*, Defoe wrote that he had counted over 2,000 sea-going vessels in the Pool of London, between Limehouse Reach and London Bridge.

For deep-sea ships, Felixstowe is conveniently near both Rotterdam and Zeebrugge. As well as the UK's largest container traffic, it has the second largest roll-on roll-off traffic, after Dover.

Until floated on the stock market in March 1996, 68.42 per cent of Orange was owned by Hutchison Whampoa and 31.58 per cent by British Aerospace.

'St Edmund's Bury' is 'the town of all this part of England, in proportion to its bigness, most thronged with gentry, people of the best fashion, and the most polite conversation', 'of which other writers have talked very largely, and perhaps a little too much'.

Ipswich is still a considerable port, probably more so than in Defoe's time, with large tonnages of cereals and animal feed, but our destination was Felixstowe, which is owned by Hutchison Whampoa, the Hong Kong group who with British Aerospace own the Orange mobile telephone network. Felixstowe handles half of all UK deep-sea container traffic, in which imports slightly outweigh exports. It is the fourth-largest container port in Europe, fifteenth in the world.

We were booked on the eleven-o'clock ferry to Zeebrugge.

Robinson said that he had to meet our employer at a
conference in Lille.

I spent a few days resting, then set off to walk along the coast
to Calais, where we had arranged to meet at the ferry.

I visited some friends I hadn't seen for several years and
spent a week-end with them at Bray-Dunes, where I lived in
the early 1970s.

In 1994, Dover's roll-on roll-off traffic was 1.18 million units. Felixstowe's was 331,000 units.

Freight through Dover has increased tenfold since 1965. Despite the Tunnel, over half the UK's international goods-vehicle traffic still passes through the port, one million vehicles per year. Nationally, roll-on roll-off traffic is about equal to that in containers, but the rate of increase has been much greater.

It is always difficult coming back to England, but we were expected in Brighton and soon forgot our *bad thoughts*.

See N. A. M. Rodger, *The Wooden World: An Anatomy of the Georgian Navy* (London, 1986), and W. D. Rubinstein, *Capitalism, Culture and Decline in Britain, 1750–1990*, which argues that Britain was never fundamentally an industrial or manufacturing economy at all.

The Supermarine Spitfire was designed by R. J. Mitchell and first flew in March 1936 at what is now Southampton Airport.

The *Titanic* was built by Harland and Wolff in Belfast and arrived at the White Star Dock at Southampton on April 4th 1912, in preparation for her maiden voyage.

The quotation is from 'Seaports', in Baudelaire's *Paris Spleen*.

In 1994, Southampton's total port traffic was 31.5 million tonnes. It is the UK's second-largest container port. The 59,093-dwt *Colombo Bay* was built in 1995, has a capacity of 4,236 teu (twenty-foot equivalent units) and is registered in London. Southampton also has a vehicle terminal, fruit and dry-bulk terminals and a lot of oil imports. The completion of the M3 at Twyford Down and the A34 Newbury bypass removed the last obstacles to rapid road access to Southampton's docks from London, the Midlands and the North.

The *Victory*, Nelson's flagship, is preserved at Portsmouth and is the principal monument of the eighteenth-century British navy, the largest industrial unit of its day in the western world, on whose supremacy was built the capitalism of land, finance and commercial services centred on the City of London, which dominates the economy of the south of England.

Those of us aesthetes who view the passing of the *visible* industrial economy with regret, and who long for an authenticity of *appearance* based on manufacturing and innovative, modern design, are inclined to view this English culture as a bizarre and damaging anachronism, but if so, it is not an unsuccessful one.

Our visit to Portsmouth coincided with that of a group of Sandhurst cadets.

In the afternoon, we visited Southampton, home port of the *Titanic*, where the Spitfire was developed and where the new 'dark' fibre optics were invented at the university.

'A seaport is a pleasant place for a soul worn out with life's struggles,' says Baudelaire. 'The wide expanse of sky, the mobile clouds, the ever changing colours of the sea . . .'

A ship like the P&O's *Colombo Bay* has a crew of twenty and carries up to 4,200 containers, each one of which may be the full load of an articulated lorry.

The M3 at Twyford Down had opened the previous October. At Newbury, the bypass had been confirmed a few days after the Tory leadership election, and people were already living in the trees.

Towards Dorchester, we passed Charborough Park.

Colonel James Drax left Yorkshire after the Civil War and settled in Barbados, where, in a few years, from £300 in sugar plantations, he acquired an estate of £8,000 to £9,000 a year.

His successor married the heiress of the Erles of Charborough.

Following the Enclosure Acts, agricultural wages in Dorset had dropped to nine shillings a week. George Loveless and others tried to get the wages increased, but they were lowered to six shillings: 'We have injured no man's reputation, character, person or property; we were uniting together to protect ourselves, our wives and our children from utter degradation and starvation.'

The manor of Charborough is mentioned in the Domesday Book as being held by the King, and remained in the King's gift for several centuries. The estate has never changed hands by sale and is unusual in that it has been repeatedly inherited by daughters. It is a private house and is not open to the public. ¶

The Tolpuddle Martyrs were the brothers George and James Loveless, James Hammett, Thomas Standfield and his son John, and James Brine. As conditions in Dorset worsened, delegates from a trade union in London were invited to Tolpuddle in October 1833. The villagers formed a friendly society, taking an oath of secrecy. One of the members turned informer; the six men were arrested and later transported to Australia. Following a national campaign, they all received conditional pardons, but were not told and did not return until 1837, when George Loveless saw a report in an old newspaper. George and James Loveless, their families and James Brine settled in Essex on an 80-acre farm bought for them by public subscription, but in 1844 all the martyrs except Hammett emigrated to Canada.

1.1 per cent of employees, 1.6 per cent of the work-force including the self-employed (from *Regional Trends* [1995 edn]). 12 per cent of employees in the south-west are in retailing, the highest proportion in the country.

With fountains worthy of Versailles, Dorchester's was the most exotic Tesco encountered during seven months of travelling.

In 1995, seven years after the project was first announced, sixty-one houses and flats – thirty-five for the Guinness Trust, twenty-six for sale – were complete or under construction as the first phase of Krier's plan for 2,000–3,000 dwellings on 400 acres to be built over twenty-five years. Krier's earlier worries that the Duchy of Cornwall was 'attempting to resist the Prince's deepest wishes in the name of financial constraints' were apparently resolved. Whatever its fate, Poundbury was one of only a very few attempts at innovation in housing provision initiated during eighteen years of Conservative government.

In England, 1.1 per cent of employees work in agriculture. In 1995 a coffee-shop assistant at Tesco earned £3.53 an hour. We very often ate in supermarkets. For the provincial spy, or anyone in a hurry who needs petrol, parking, telephone, postal services, clean toilets and *palatable* food, there is really no practical alternative.

On the other side of Dorchester is Poundbury – the project of the Prince of Wales – which, with the magazine *Perspectives* and the Institute of Architecture, is the outcome of his ten-year opposition to contemporary architecture.

The project was planned, apparently with some difficulties, by the architect Leon Krier and has been executed by the Percy Thomas Partnership of Cardiff.

Our arrival in Yeovil coincided with that of Tim Eggar, the Trade and Industry minister at the time, who was to announce that Westland had been awarded a £2.5-billion order to build American attack helicopters for the army, in preference to the domestic options offered by British Aerospace and GEC.

Westland is now owned by GKN.

For the rest of the day, we looked at some non-agricultural land uses.

We knew of six Jane Austen film or television adaptations under way, all involving country houses, mostly in the west of England. *Sense and Sensibility* was made at Montacute.

We called at Worthy Farm, near Glastonbury, where the Festival site was being cleared, and Halecombe Quarry at Leigh-upon-Mendip.

The DoE believes that the demand for aggregates could more than double in the next twenty years.

This choice, criticized as a decision to buy American, was the first taken by Michael Portillo as defence secretary.

The 'Westland Affair' in 1986 began as a choice between a Sikorsky-Fiat collaboration or a European consortium (British Aerospace, GEC, Aérospatiale, Agusta and Messerschmidt-Bölkow-Blohm) preferred by Michael Heseltine to rescue the ailing company. The Cabinet crisis which precipitated Heseltine's resignation was based on the perception of Sikorsky-Fiat as a move towards American ownership. In fact, when this option went ahead, Sikorsky owned only 7 per cent and Fiat 20 per cent of Westland shares, the majority being held, as before, by 'a small number of institutional investors'.

The Austen adaptations were BBC2's *Persuasion*, BBC1's *Pride and Prejudice*, Columbia's *Sense and Sensibility*, Miramax's *Emma*, and two more *Emma*s, two hours for ITV and five parts for BBC1.

The 1995 Glastonbury Festival was the busiest ever, a Brit-pop showcase with both Oasis and Pulp performing.

The Mendip Hills are apparently the most heavily quarried area in Europe.

97

On July 14th, we reached the Bristol Channel.

We were expected at the Portbury Dock.

Bristol imports more cars than any other port in the UK and had the best PR of any port we visited: 'Bristol is closer to the enormous markets of the Americas, Australia and the Pacific Rim than any other port in the UK. The Port of Bristol is the only major UK port to employ a permanent workforce.'

There were 60,000 cars at Portbury, ready for the new registration year on August 1st, including many Daewoos from South Korea, new on the UK market.

Two weeks later, we came back again, to visit the automated plasterboard factory and the coal stockyard, to which materials are conveyed directly from the ships.

The coal is mostly from Richard's Bay, in South Africa, and is carried to power stations by train.

The Port of Bristol includes the docks at Avonmouth and the Royal Portbury Dock, on either side of the mouth of the River Avon. Portbury was completed in 1978. In 1995, it imported cars for Toyota, Honda, Mitsubishi, Subaru, Isuzu, Hyundai, Daewoo, Proton, Fiat, Alfa Romeo, General Motors and Ford, and exported for Rover, General Motors and Honda. Portbury had the most imports, but with more exports Sheerness handled slightly more cars. Portbury also has 'the most advanced bulk-handling terminal in Europe', a computer-controlled facility which unloads animal feeds, fertilizers, aggregates, coal and coke. National Power's coal terminal is connected to the railhead in Avonmouth by a conveyor link which runs under the River Avon.

All UK species of owl are now resident on the Bristol Port Company site, including the first recorded recolonization by the barn owl.

Captain Rogers, the
commander of the ships
Duke and *Duchess,* whose
Voyage Round the World
(1712) relates the rescue of
Alexander Selkirk, built a
house at 19 Queen Square
nearby. Burke stayed
there in 1774 during his
successful election
campaign.

The Llandoger Trow was
one of the last timber-
framed buildings to be
built in Bristol, in 1664.
It is also said to be the
inspiration for the Spy
Glass, in Stevenson's
Treasure Island.

Part 1 of *After London* was
broadcast by BBC Radio 4
during July 1995 in five
fifteen-minute readings by
Paul Scofield.

The British Aerospace site
at Filton is the largest
military aircraft factory
in Europe.

In Bristol, we visited the Llandoger Trow, where Defoe is supposed to have met Alexander Selkirk, the real Robinson Crusoe.

A Llandoger Trow was a boat which carried coal to Bristol from South Wales.

In Richard Jefferies's *After London,* the *red rocks* of Bristol are the western extremity of the lake which has covered most of southern England, and the Severn has silted up.

Robinson had been most affected by this book, which we had heard one night being read on the radio and had mistaken for a documentary.

On what was then the hottest day of the year, we walked out on the Severn Bridge.

In the afternoon, we visited Filton.

Our employer had given Robinson a copy of *Capitalism, Culture and Decline in Britain, 1750–1990*, by W. D. Rubinstein, who notes the 'close and harmonious connection (before 1832) between City finance, land, the professions, and the *government* as contractor, loan agent, and originator of "Old Corruption", the extraordinary system of lucrative perquisites which came to fortunate aristocrats, government employees and their relatives.

'The British government itself acted as the central matrix of this system, directly through contracts and perquisites, indirectly by maintaining British control of the seas, the Empire and the balance of power.'

The Ministry of Defence's Abbey Wood headquarters for the 4,300 civil servants of its Procurement Executive cost £254 million and include 230 bathrooms, a gymnasium, landscaped gardens and a lake on 98 acres about five kilometres north of Bristol. Following criticism, the Ministry claimed that its move there in December 1995 would save £100 million a year through staff cuts made possible by the new single location.

The Abbey Wood headquarters were designed by the Percy Thomas Partnership, founded in Cardiff in 1912 and once one of the biggest architects' practices in the south-western UK. The building won the 1997 Green Building of the Year Award. Percy Thomas Partnership were architects for the Severn Bridge, which opened in 1966, co-ordinating architects for the Prince of Wales's Poundbury development and designers of the Welsh Millennium Centre in Cardiff Bay following the rejection of the competition-winning design by Zaha Hadid. Other controversial projects involved the decommissioning of the Trawsfynydd nuclear power station and the building of an orimulsion-burning plant at Pembroke Dock. In September 1997, the practice obtained the agreement of its creditors for a company voluntary arrangement to pay off its debts, without which it would have had to cease trading.

In 1994, the combined annual budget of MI6 and GCHQ was officially estimated at £900 million, the bulk of it spent on GCHQ, which employed 6,000 civilians and 3,000 armed forces personnel, compared with about 2,000 at MI6. Lord Mackay said that the intelligence agencies kept 'a particular eye on Britain's access to key commodities, like oil or metals . . . the profits of Britain's myriad of international business interests . . . are dependent on the ability to plan, to invest, and to trade effectively without worry. . .'

The DERA at Malvern was previously the Telecommunications Research Establishment, which moved to the present site in 1946. Before that, it was the Royal Signals and Radar Establishment, which developed radar before World War Two. Microwave ovens and liquid-crystal displays originated from research at Malvern. Most of the DERA's work is for the Ministry of Defence, but it also develops and markets electronic equipment for air-traffic control, firefighting and other applications. In March 1998 George Robertson, the defence secretary, proposed a defence diversification agency within the DERA to improve the UK's poor record in commercial exploitation of its military research.

See Letter 6 of Defoe's *Tour*. Silver was discovered at Potosi in Peru in 1545.

'Britain's role as the world's fifth-largest trading nation is essential for its economic well-being,' said Lord Mackay, the Lord Chancellor, during the first reading of the intelligence services bill in 1993. It was very hot.

The Defence Evaluation and Research Agency, at Malvern, is a world centre for liquid crystals development and semi-conductor research.

'They talk much of mines of gold and silver,' said Defoe, 'which are certainly to be found here, if they were but looked for, and that Mauvern would outdo Potosi . . .'

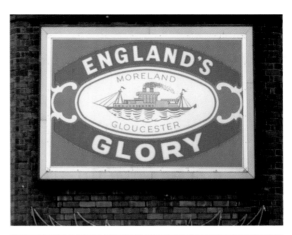

It was the driest summer since records began.

We wanted to have a look at Blakenhurst Prison, near Redditch, run by UK Detention Services, one of six *Bullingdon*-type prisons based on an original design by Building Design Partnership.

Merry Hill, near Dudley, is the largest shopping centre in Europe. More than 4.5 million people are within a sixty-five-minute drive.

It is connected to the nearby Waterfront development by a monorail, though this was not operating on the day of our visit. At the top of the hill are the offices of the Child Support Agency.

The Waterfront and Merry Hill were built on the site of the former Round Oak steelworks.

Merry Hill attracts 25 million shopping visits a year, and its effects are felt in towns 200 miles away.

In the end, the summer was the second driest.

Merry Hill was developed after 1986 by former scrap dealers and twin brothers Don and Roy Richardson on land within the Dudley Enterprise Zone, designated in 1981, and the Dudley (Round Oak) Enterprise Zone, which came into operation in 1984. The Round Oak steelworks closed in 1982, having been founded by the Earl of Dudley in 1857 as an outlet for pig iron made in his nearby blast furnaces. During the early nineteenth century, the majority of iron-making in the world was carried out within thirty-two kilometres of Round Oak.

In 1997, Merry Hill was the largest shopping mall in the UK, with 168,000 square metres of retail space in 225 shops.

The Waterfront is another development by the Richardson twins in the manner of the London Docklands, with offices, distribution depots, neoclassical architecture, Italian restaurants and business hotels. Michael Portillo opened a bridge across the Waterfront's lake when he was Treasury chief secretary, and the Child Support Agency's offices and a further phase of offices when he was Employment secretary in 1994.

Robinson wanted to visit Halesowen, to see the factory where the Supergun parts had been produced.

We were both ill from the cumulative effects of months of bad food and living in hotels, and were becoming seriously worried about the weather.

Robinson imagined the entire landscape occupied in manufacturing goods for export to the Middle East.

The West Midlands are traditionally the region where elections are decided.

In 1990, Walter Somers Ltd belonged to Eagle Trust, which was finally wound up in December 1997. In January 1990, on a visit to the factory, 'company doctor' David James noticed three large steel pipes, which the company believed were for an Iraqi petrochemical plant, and contacted MI6. The pipes were at Tees Dock when their export was stopped by customs officers.

Walter Somers Ltd was taken over by the Folkes Group plc in 1990, and is now known as Somers Forge. They manufacture forgings such as crank-shafts, up to a maximum weight of 45 tons.

August 1995 was the hottest month since temperature records began in 1659.

In the Dudley West by-election the previous December, Labour's winning share of the vote had been their biggest in any by-election in a Tory seat since 1933.

On August 11th, we reached West Bromwich, where we had come to see the headquarters of Hyundai UK, which is part-owned by a company called International Motors.

Their Phoenix-International industrial estate is next to the factory of Phoenix Drawn Tube.

In an essay by the geographer Doreen Massey, we had read: '. . . amid the Ridley Scott images of world cities, the writing about skyscraper fortresses, the Baudrillard visions of hyperspace . . . most people actually still live in places like Harlesden or West Brom.'

Across the road is a chemical manufacturing company called Robinson Brothers.

There are watercolours of Dudley by Turner in the Lady Lever Art Gallery at Port Sunlight on Merseyside, painted in 1830 for his series *Picturesque Views of England and Wales.*

Hyundai UK is owned 50.1 per cent by Lex Services, 49.9 per cent by International Motors. IM have the sole import rights to Subaru, Isuzu and SsangYong. The IM group was founded by former employees of the failed Jensen Motors, which made luxury sports cars. The phoenix in the Phoenix-International name is symbolic of the new company rising from the ashes of the old and has no connection with its neighbour Phoenix Drawn Tube.

The quotation is from 'A Place called Home?' in *Space, Place and Gender* (Cambridge, 1994), p. 163.

Robinson Brothers produce chemicals including organics, accelerators and pharmaceuticals. The company was established on its present site in the late 1800s, and a second plant opened in Newcastle uponTyne in the 1960s.

113

The Clock Tower's architect (*c.* 1897) was Edward Pincher, and it was given to the town by Richard Farley, who was five times mayor of West Bromwich. The other three faces of the plinth have terracotta panels showing images of the town hall, Farley's residence Oak House, and Farley himself.

Robinson introduced himself to the managing director and explained our project, and we were very generously looked after for the next two weeks while we convalesced.

'Much of life for many people,' read Robinson, 'even in the heart of the First World, still consists of waiting in a bus shelter with your shopping for a bus that never comes.'

The bus shelter was opposite the premises of Smallman Lubricants.

When the bus finally arrived, Robinson had disappeared, to a sexual encounter with a stranger he had contacted through the Internet while we were waiting at the bus-stop.

Our employer had equipped us with a notebook computer and a mobile phone.

In the eighteenth century, Birmingham made fetters, chains, padlocks, branding irons and other equipment, as well as copper wire, iron bars, pans, kettles, guns and other goods which were bartered for slaves.

In 1983, two reporters from the *Daily Mirror* posing as potential buyers were offered leg-irons, gang-chains and other restraining equipment. Following a campaign by Amnesty International and others, the government announced that export licences 'would not be issued for the export to any destination of leg-irons, shackles and gang-chains specifically designed for restraining prisoners. Applications for export licences for other purposes – for example, for theatrical performances or museum display – will be considered on their merits.' In 1991, at the COPEX exhibition in Miami, two human-rights workers were given a brochure advertising leg-cuffs available from Hiatt-Thompson, a US-registered company. The brochure stated that the equipment was made in Birmingham, England.

The car in the top picture is a Morris Marina, which would have been produced at Cowley in the 1970s. The Marina 'might well have been launched as "the unexportable motor car"' (see Karel Williams *et al.*, *Cars: Analysis, History, Cases* [Providence, 1994], pp. 157–60). A few years earlier, the 1100 had explicitly been launched as a 'world car'.

We walked over to the Hiatt works, in Great Barr.

Hiatt is one of the oldest firms in Birmingham, established in 1780, in the era of the slave trade, who make handcuffs and other items, and whose name recently still appeared on leg-irons used in Saudi prisons. Robinson went in and bought a pair of handcuffs.

Beneath Spaghetti Junction, we met a man with a dog who said he had been paid for denouncing illegal emigrants who had been working on repairs to the structure.

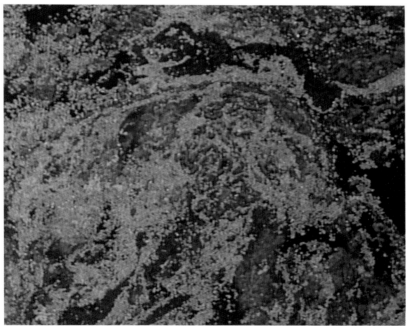

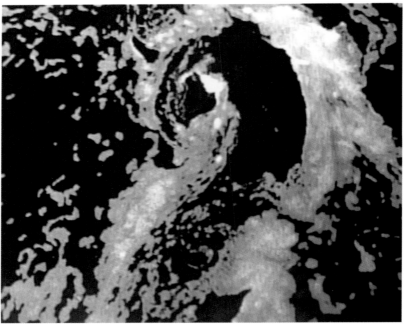

We were very relieved to reach the Jaguar body plant, at Castle Bromwich, where Ford had secured government investment for the X200 small saloon.

This is the factory where thousands of Spitfires were built during World War Two.

The next day, we left Birmingham.

Neither of us knows anything about Johnson, except that *The Anatomy of Melancholy* 'was the only book that ever took him out of bed two hours earlier than he wanted to rise . . .'

We crossed the River Trent at Burton, where we stayed the night and woke up very early.

The Swallow Sidecar Company was formed by William Lyons and William Walmsley in September 1922 in Blackpool. After several successful adaptations of production cars and a move to Coventry, it launched the SSI and SSII Coupés in 1931. The company became successful by creating products that were *not as expensive as they looked*. In 1935, when the SS Jaguar 2.5-litre saloon was unveiled and those present were asked to guess its price, the average guess was £632. The actual price was £395. After the war, the SS name was dropped and the company became Jaguar Cars Ltd.

The huge 'shadow' factory at Castle Bromwich was part of an Air Ministry programme to increase aircraft production. In 1939, the first contract was placed for the production of a thousand Spitfires. Production commenced in June 1940, and Castle Bromwich became the largest source of the 22,000 Spitfires and Seafires produced, with a maximum output of nearly 350 aircraft a month in 1943.

In 1995, Tesco, Sainsbury, Morrisons and Safeway all had large superstores in Burton-on-Trent. Burton was then the point of contact between northward-expanding Tesco and southward-expanding Morrisons.

In March 1995, Toyota
confirmed its plans to
double output at its
Burnaston plant to
200,000 cars a year, adding
1,000 jobs to the 1,900
already at the plant, which
was then producing the
Carina E model.

Rolls-Royce is Europe's
largest aero-engine maker.
The City was reported to
have judged that an
underlying fall in profit
had been masked by a
£28 million cut in research-
and-development spending
and £23 million from
disposals in the company's
Industrial Power Group.
This provides design,
manufacturing, etc. for
power generation and
transmission, oil and gas,
marine propulsion and
materials handling. In
1995, it employed 17,000
people and had an annual
turnover of £1.2 billion. In
March 1996, the chairman
predicted that further
progress would depend
on the pace of restructuring
– alliances and closures –
amongst European
engine-builders.

Four D's Supatex is a
natural latex-rubber sheet
specially formulated for
making rubber fashion
clothing. Four D's factory is
in Slack Lane, Heanor, on
the Heanor Gate Industrial
Estate.

Robin Hood's Well is about
2.5 kilometres north-east of
Eastwood, in a wood
alongside the M1 motorway.
The land is owned by the
Barker family, who are
apparently wary of media
interest, having been
portrayed unfavourably by
D. H. Lawrence.

The day we arrived in Derby, Rolls-Royce announced
half-year profits up 43 per cent to £70 million, though the
chairman would not rule out more job losses, and the
shares fell 8 per cent.

'The English are acknowledged world leaders in fetishism
and S&M,' Robinson read in the paper. 'The only company in
the world that makes latex sheeting suitable for fetishwear is
based in Derbyshire . . .'

We wanted to visit Robin Hood's Well, near Eastwood, but
the wood had been fenced off by the owner.

We did not go any further in this direction.

We turned towards the north-west and the next morning set
off towards Liverpool, following the Derwent valley.

Tesco is still expanding in the north of England. The distribution centre at Middlewich holds 43 million cases, about nine days' stock for 120 stores, and delivers as far away as Gateshead. Six more superstores were scheduled to open in the north by May 1997.

East Mill was built in 1912. Belper's water-powered South, North and West mills were built by Jebediah Strutt in 1778, 1786 and 1795. Until 1780, Strutt was in partnership with Richard Arkwright, with whom he built the world's first water-powered cotton-spinning mill in 1771 at Cromford, higher up the valley.

Riber Castle was built in 1862 as a private house by John Smedley, the knitwear manufacturer. Smedley's mill, at Lea Bridge, near the first Strutt and Arkwright mill at Cromford, is still in operation. Riber Castle is now a shell, surrounded by a wildlife park established in 1962.

The realization of Thomas the Tank Engine on page 124 is on a siding at the Peak Rail Line's Darley Dale station, north of Matlock.

The Jodrell Bank radio telescope came into use in 1957 and was celebrated when in October of that year it was able to receive the bleeps of the Soviet Sputnik satellite.

Tesco's distribution centre at Midpoint opened in June 1993 and covers 37,500 square metres. In 1995, Tesco had 545 stores in England, Scotland and Wales, 110 in France, forty-five in Hungary and newly acquired chains in Poland, the Czech Republic and Slovakia.

Liverpool is the major UK port for trade with the eastern seaboard of North America. It has a successful container terminal, imports more grain than any other UK port, handles most of the UK's scrap-metal exports and a lot of oil, and has a new terminal for Powergen's coal imports. With the opening of the Channel Tunnel, Liverpool was able to market itself as a mainland European port for north Atlantic traffic, and there are daily rail-freight services to cities as far away as Milan (32 hours) and Vienna (34 hours). In 1995, the MDHC was ranked 253rd in the *Financial Times*'s top 500 UK companies, and 13.9 per cent of its shares were owned by the Treasury. ¶

In 1995, Powergen sponsored the ITV weather forecast with the slogan 'Generating electricity whatever the weather'. In 1994, there were reports that coal was coming into Liverpool from Colombian mines worked by child labour. According to McCloskey Coal Information Services, there were children working in small mines near Bogota, but Powergen's coal came from other mines near the coast. Another industry source suggested that it might be difficult to be this precise about the sources of Colombian coal.

On September 4th, we arrived in Liverpool.

In the statistics for 1993, the Mersey Dock and Harbour Company was the most profitable of any port authority listed.

In the last 30 years, Liverpool's traffic has fluctuated more than that of any other UK port. It is now about the same as in 1965, three times more than in the early '80s, and Liverpool is one of the biggest ports in England.

Liverpool imports coal for Powergen from the USA and Colombia and exports enormous tonnages of scrap, mostly to the Far East and Spain.

The company did not want us to photograph the scrap. Not long after our visit, they sacked 329 dock workers for refusing to cross a picket-line.

When dockers in New York began secondary protests, the ACL container line said it would leave Liverpool unless the lock-out there was ended, and the Mersey company's share value dropped by £70 million.

The biggest shareholder in the Mersey Dock and Harbour Company is the Treasury.

The company's safety officer would not say why he didn't want us to photograph the scrap within the MDHC site, but a local journalist suggested that it might have been because there were occasional fires in the scrap, and there had been fears of PCB emissions. The view is from the road.

Our next appointments were in Warrington: the Thorn Cross young-offender institution, which had been chosen to become the first US-style 'boot camp', and the KinderCare nursery, the first to open in the UK.

KinderCare runs over a thousand centres in thirty-eight American states.

Warrington is near the crossing point of two motorways and has attracted many large distribution centres.

We stayed the night in a Whitbread Travel Inn near Wigan which had opened the previous week. Our rooms were quite new – no-one had ever stayed in them before . . .

The Liverpool and Manchester Railway opened on September 15th 1830. Robinson took me to see the memorial to William Huskisson, the Cabinet minister who was knocked down by the *Rocket* as it passed the dignitaries gathered for the occasion.

In September 1995, Paul Cavadino of the Penal Affairs Consortium said that the boot-camp regime would 'combine a hard physical approach, which will do nothing to reduce offending, with some constructive elements of rehabilitation, which could do so'.

KinderCare spent three years researching the UK market and discovered the lowest level of pre-school provision in Europe. In 1995, the company had a target of establishing between fifty and a hundred centres over five years.

Warrington's status as a major location for distribution and retailing was confirmed in the 1980s when the first IKEA store in the UK opened there.

In 1995, on payment of £34.50 at a Travel Inn, one gained entry to a surprisingly large room, with a large and comfortable double bed, desk, sofa, chairs, TV etc., room to walk about, and a bathroom with pumped hot water and a proper shower. There was no telephone (though there were several in the corridor), mini-bar or anything else that required payment the next morning. The room could sleep up to four adults and a baby. ¶

Huskisson and others had got down from the state carriage when it stopped for its locomotive to take on water. ¶¶

135

In the picture at the bottom of page 137, the signs in front of houses on the A49 (Winwick Road) are protesting against the development of the former colliery site. British Coal, primarily a landowner after its surviving pits were privatized, had invited Morrisons to propose a depot to serve their stores between Carlisle and Cardiff as the start of a larger redevelopment. Parkside is not far from the M6–M62 junction and next to the main London–Glasgow railway line, but is in a primarily residential area, and the local road access is poor. The planning authority, St Helens, was supportive as the developers estimated that the development would produce 2,000 jobs – more than the 1,700 lost when the colliery was closed – but the proposal was turned down following a public inquiry. In May 1998, British Coal's successor, the Coal Authority, was preparing to sell the colliery site to the highest bidder.

Latchford was not an official boarding point, though the lock keepers still recall that it was not that uncommon for people to arrive by taxi and board their ship at the locks. The journey from Salford to the last lock at Eastham takes about six hours, so there is plenty of scope for this. The Ship Canal was opened in 1894. There was slightly more traffic in 1995 than there had been in 1988, the time of a previous visit.

British Coal closed Parkside Colliery in 1993 and cleared the site after an eighteen-month-long women's protest vigil. They proposed a massive distribution centre for Morrisons' supermarkets, with 5,000 vehicle movements daily.

The coal used to go by train to Fiddler's Ferry power station, which is now supplied from the terminal we had seen in Liverpool docks.

We had lunch in a brand-new Marks & Spencer on the edge of Warrington.

Robinson told me he had a relative who had emigrated to Canada from Warrington in 1935. He had walked to the locks at Latchford and boarded one of the Manchester Liners which sailed to the Great Lakes until the late '70s.

As *the* major contributor to 'the end of work', Turing seems at home in a Manchester famous for industrial ruins, dance music, the pink pound, latterday Situationism and science fiction. 'Alan Turing was largely responsible for developing one of the most important technologies of the 20th century,' wrote Dr Peter Mowforth of Glasgow University's Turing Institute in May 1996. 'If he had been an American, they would have named a city after him; as it is, we have part of a ring road.'

The brothers Adam and George Murray arrived in Manchester from southern Scotland in the 1780s. They established a successful business as textile-machinery makers and cotton spinners in a number of mills around Manchester before concentrating on fine-cotton spinning at the Ancoats site, alongside the Rochdale Canal. The original part of Murray's Mills comprises four mills built between 1798 and 1806, including Old Mill, the last mill to survive from Manchester's boom in factory building in the late 1790s.

Friedrich Engels arrived in Manchester in 1842, when he was twenty-two. He came from a wealthy family of cotton manufac-turers in the Rhineland that had established a branch in Manchester. He stayed in England for almost two years. By 1844, he was at work on the book; most of the writing was done in the winter of 1844–5.

We arrived in Manchester on September 19th.

In 1937, Turing published his paper 'On Computable Numbers'.

Two years later, he joined the Code and Cypher School at Bletchley Park, in the team which cracked the German navy's Enigma code, so that convoys could dodge U-boats in the north Atlantic. He continued his computer work at Manchester University, becoming director of the Manchester Automatic Digital Machine. In 1954, a police investigation of a burglary at his home led to his being charged with gross indecency. He pleaded guilty and was put on probation on condition that he submitted to hormone treatment. Shortly afterwards, he killed himself by eating an apple impregnated with cyanide. He was forty-two.

Murray's mill in Ancoats was built in 1798. It is the world's oldest steam-driven mill, and as such is described as 'the first factory'.

Engels visited Ancoats frequently in 1842, while working for the firm of Ermen and Engels in Manchester.

His *Condition of the Working Class in England* was published in 1845 in Leipzig, but not in Britain until 1892.

The John Milne Brewers Fayre and its Travel Inn at Milnrow, next to the M62 near Rochdale, were built on farmland once owned by the Milne family. ¶

In September 1995, the level in North West Water's Blackstone Edge Reservoir was very low. At the time, North West Water was criticized by the National Rivers Authority for failing to ban non-essential water use before applying for a drought order to take extra water from rivers, and by its regional customer-service committee for its handling of its worst-ever supply crisis.

Two major National Grid transmission lines converge near Blackstone Edge Reservoir. In 1989, the CEGB (as it then was) applied to build taller and wider pylons, as the originals from the 1950s had corroded, but planning permission was not granted and instead the corroded parts of the original pylons were replaced.

In June 1995, Yorkshire Water announced that its operating profits were up almost a fifth to £200 million, put up its dividend by 21 per cent and gave its consumers a £10 rebate in an attempt to counter two years of bad publicity while losing at least 27 per cent of its supplies through leaks. The company's directors had previously awarded themselves £869,000 in share options. ¶ ¶

We stayed in another Travel Inn at Milnrow near Rochdale, which had been open for about a month. These places always seemed to be hosting conferences for their own executives.

John Milne was a civil engineer with a passion for volcanoes. He travelled overland to Tokyo, where he was Professor of Geology and Mining, and developed the seismograph. He wrote many books, including some science fiction.

We had ascended the Pennines at Blackstone Edge, by the route of Daniel Defoe.

When we arrived at Yorkshire Water's reservoir near Ripponden, there were twenty-four tankers waiting to load water to be taken into Halifax.

At the time, there were altogether forty lorries working from this reservoir, twenty-four hours a day.

Later in the year, there were as many as a thousand tankers moving water in West Yorkshire.

Yorkshire Windpower's
Ovenden Moor Windfarm
is a joint project of
Yorkshire Electricity and
Yorkshire Water, who own
the land. It began operating
in 1993 and comprises
twenty-three wind turbines
manufactured in Denmark
by Vestas – Danish Wind
Technology A/S ; these
turbines generate 9.2 mw,
enough electricity for about
7,500 homes. Planning
permission for the wind
farm was granted in 1992
following a public inquiry.
Sir Bernard Ingham, who
was Margaret Thatcher's
press secretary, lives
nearby at Hebden Bridge.
An adviser to British
Nuclear Fuels Ltd, he is a
prominent opponent
of wind farms and vice-
president of Country
Guardian, a pressure
group. In 1996, the UK had
550 wind turbines, about
10 per cent of Europe's
total, although the UK has
an estimated 40 per cent of
Europe's potential wind
power.

The leak in the picture at
the bottom of page 147 was
at the junction of Queen's
Road and Gibbet Street, in
Halifax.

Near the treatment works in Halifax, someone told us where
they'd just seen another leak, so we went and had a look.

We had an appointment at the wind farm on Ovenden Moor,
above the town.

We are both very fond of Halifax. It was the first place we'd had a decent cup of coffee in months.

At Saltaire, north of Bradford, Pace Microtechnology make digital television equipment for export to the Far East and Australasia.

Defoe's description of the Pennine cloth manufacture of which Halifax was then the centre is in Letter 8 of his *Tour*. The later Piece Hall cloth market – a two-tier square-plan stone construction completed in 1779 – is in the lower centre of the picture on page 150, behind the steeple which is all that survives of the Square Congregational Church.

Pace occupy part of Salt's Mill, at Sir Titus Salt's model village of Saltaire alongside the River Aire. Pace was founded in 1982 when Ferguson moved its manufacturing capacity to Gosport. A number of engineers decided to stay in Bradford, and Pace made its first satellite receiver in 1987. Between 1990 and 1994, the company's turnover rose to £107 million, but it remained in private ownership to protect its research and development from shareholder pressure until June 1996, when it was floated on the stock market. In February 1997, the company's shares slumped following two profits warnings, the departure of one of the co-founders and uncertainty over whether Pace would receive orders to make satellite decoders for BSkyB. It subsequently received orders from both BSkyB and British Digital Broadcasting.

The Lister Mill at Manningham, Bradford, was completed in 1873 and became the biggest silk and velvet manufacturing centre in the world; a strike in 1890–91 hastened the Labour movement's entry into politics. Jonathan Silver first suggested moving the Victoria and Albert Museum's South Indian collection to Bradford, and in 1988 the V&A were considering the Lister Mill, Salt's Mill and a site in Bradford's shopping centre. In 1996, the museum was still looking for a regional base, but in Sheffield.

Quarry House, the £55-million base of the Benefits Agency and the NHS Executive, includes computer-controlled water displays, a swimming pool, squash courts, a gym and a sports hall. It was included in a sell-off of DSS buildings announced in June 1996 which aimed to raise £4 billion for the Treasury to preserve scope for pre-election tax cuts threatened by the expected £2 billion cost of mad cow disease.

In the bottom picture on page 153 are a Showcase Cinema multiplex, a Pizza Hut, a McDonald's and a Currys store. In November 1997, First Leisure, the owner of Blackpool Tower, chaired by Michael Grade, opened the 2,000-capacity Club Barcelona, one of a chain of out-of-town super-clubs.

The V&A never managed to move their South Indian collection to the Lister Mill in Bradford, but the police station is new.

In Leeds, the site of the famous Quarry Hill flats is now occupied by the Department of Social Security.

'Junction 27' is a leisure park. 'Wakefield 41' is a distribution estate where Morrisons have their depots.

On the threshold of our century, Henri Bergson wrote: 'If reality could immediately reach our senses and our consciousness, if we could come into direct contact with things and with each other, probably art would be useless, or rather we should all be artists . . .'

While we were in Wakefield, Robinson met someone who told him that Bergson's mother had come from Doncaster . . .

There are three prisons in Doncaster. The largest is run by a subsidiary of the American Wackenhut Corporation. It has the cheapest cost per prisoner in the UK, a non-union staff and a record of violence and chaos. Doncaster Prison was designed by Seifert Limited.

Some of Morrisons' trucks carry a large 'M', some the name 'William Morrison – the Potato King', others 'Household Potatoes Ltd'. In 1997, the Bradford-based company was almost a hundred years old and had expanded during the 1990s as far south as the Midlands. There were plans to open superstores in Erith, Banbury and Letchworth, and for the distribution depot at Parkside, north of Warrington.

The Bergson quotation is from his essay 'Laughter', reprinted in *Comedy*, edited by Wylie Sypher (Baltimore and London, 1980). Bergson was born in 1859 in Paris, the son of Catherine Levison, of Doncaster, and Michel Bergson, a composer and pianist who lived in France, Switzerland and, finally, England. Bergson's parents left Paris for Geneva, where his father was for a time director of the Conservatory, when Bergson was four, and settled in London when he was eleven. He visited them in the school holidays. After the death of her husband, his mother lived in Folkestone; she died there aged ninety-eight. See Madeleine Barthelemy-Madaule, *Bergson* (Paris, 1967).

The prisons in Doncaster are: Doncaster Prison, 'core local' – category B and some category A prisoners; Lindholme Prison, category B; Moorland, category C and Young Offender Institution. Hatfield Young Offender Institution is also in Doncaster. ¶

Bentley used to be one of the most left-wing pits in Yorkshire. When it closed, it was producing the UK's cheapest coal, undercutting even Colombian imports. There were 600,000 tonnes stockpiled at the pit.

RJB own seventeen of the thirty-one surviving pits and had contracts with the power generators until 1998.

There are 7,000 miners still working in the industry, 1 per cent of the number in 1946.

The advancement of Stella Rimington, MI5's former director, followed her role directing sabotage of the miners' strike, and the *amateur* interventions of David Hart, old Etonian and former bankrupt, began with his funding strike-breaking miners. In 1995, he was unpaid adviser to Michael Portillo at the Ministry of Defence.

A third of all UK deep-mined coal is burnt at Drax. Hugo Drax was James Bond's opponent in *Moonraker*.

In 1913, total production of coal in the UK was 287.4 million tons; there were 1.16 million working in the industry, 830,000 of them underground. Coal production dropped below 200 million tonnes after 1962 and below 100 million after 1988. In 1994, it was 48 million tonnes, of which 31 million were deep-mined and the rest from open-cast sites. Imports of coal rose from almost none before 1969 to about 4.5 million tonnes in 1983 and then rapidly after the 1984–5 miners' strike. In 1992, over 20 million tonnes were imported, and just under 1 million exported.

In October 1992, Michael Heseltine announced plans to close thirty-one of British Coal's surviving fifty-one pits and cut 30,000 jobs. Following electricity privatization, distributors were obliged to use nuclear-generated electricity for 'base-load' and were encouraged to build gas-fired power stations, with supply contracts under which gas had to be paid for whether it was used or not. Demand for coal fell and pits were closed despite the UK's having 200 years of reserves and coal being a commodity for which global demand was rising.¶

Drax is western Europe's largest coal-fired power station, with a maximum output of 4,000 mw. Owned by National Power, it consumes over 10 million tonnes of coal a year, the entire production of the nearby Selby coalfield.¶¶

On October 5th, we entered the network area of Kingston Communications, on the north bank of the Humber.

Kingston Communications is owned, through the city council, by the citizens of Hull.

Robinson took me to the fish dock. He had read how the navy used to recruit trawlermen as unpaid spies.

Daniel Defoe was happy to welcome William III to England.

This statue was erected in the year 1734: 'To the Memory of KING WILLIAM the THIRD, OUR GREAT DELIVERER'.

Robinson and I are proud to recollect our own experiences of *The Glorious Revolution*.

Robinson Crusoe sailed from Hull on September 1st 1651.

Kingston Communications have invested in a satellite and has a worker-director on its board. William Wilberforce was born in Hull in 1759.

The Hull Telephone Department was founded by the city council in 1904. In 1987, it changed its name to Kingston Communications. Eight of its twelve board members are city councillors, and it contributes 40 per cent of profits to municipal social projects.

In 1966, Hull landed about 200,000 tonnes of fish, some 20 per cent of the UK's consumption. In 1992, Hull's fleet of nineteen vessels caught 54,000 tonnes, 9,500 tonnes landed at Hull and the rest elsewhere. During the Cold War, Hull trawlers carried naval intelligence officers; radio operators were issued with monitoring equipment and skippers given cameras. ¶

The statue of William III in Hull was originally intended for Bristol. It was paid for by public subscription. ¶¶

Robinson Crusoe begins: 'I was born in the year 1632, in the city of York, of a good family, tho' not of that country, my father being a foreigner of Bremen, who settled first at Hull. . . and leaving off his trade lived afterward at York, from whence he had married my mother, whose relations were named Robinson, a very good family in that country, and from whom I was called Robinson Kreutznaer; but by the usual corruption of words in England, we are now called, nay, we call our selves and write our name, Crusoe, and so my companions always called me.'

In 1965, Hull's port traffic was 9.4 million tonnes. It fell to a low point of 3.6 million tonnes in 1979, but by 1994 was 10.2 million tonnes, half of which was container and roll-on roll-off traffic. There are daily ferry services to Rotterdam and Zeebrugge, and others to Finland, Hamburg and St Petersburg.

Between 1881 and 1897, the Medical Officer of Health's annual reports record that 775,272 emigrants arrived at Hull from Europe. Otherwise, there seem to be no records of arrivals – until August 1914 anyone could live in Britain without a permit – but the Merseyside Maritime Museum estimate that between 1830 and 1930, about ten million people left Liverpool for North America. Most of these were English, Scots or Irish, but there were Scandinavians, Jewish emigrants from Russia and Eastern Europe and others. After the 1920s, European emigration was more likely to be from Dutch or Belgian ports.

Hull is the eastern English port on the Dublin-to-Berlin motorway. In the last century, the traffic was the other way, as more than a million emigrants from Central and Eastern Europe passed through the port on their way to Liverpool and the New World. Many settled in Yorkshire, including perhaps the Levisons, whose daughter Catherine was Henri Bergson's mother.

We crossed the estuary to Immingham.

Immingham is managed jointly with Grimsby by Associated British Ports. Grimsby's traffic includes imports from Volkswagen and exports from Toyota. The much greater traffic at Immingham includes imports of oil for the Immingham refineries and chemicals into and out of quayside plants. Apart from this, there are some container and conventional traffic, and car imports.

British Aerospace's site at Brough is the factory of the former Blackburn Aeroplane Company, whose last production aircraft was the Buccaneer. Blackburn became part of Hawker Siddeley, which later became part of British Aerospace. The Hawk is BAe's money-spinner; about 700 have been sold since 1972. The RAF and the US Navy have about 170 each. The world's leading fast jet trainer, the Hawk was developed as a cheap defence and ground-attack aircraft. The aircraft are not constructed entirely at Brough: they are carried across the Pennines by road for final assembly and flight testing at Warton on the Ribble estuary. In April 1996, the Indonesian air force began negotiating with BAe to buy twenty Hawks to add to the twenty it already had, making Indonesia the third-largest customer for the aircraft.

To *materialists* like us, Immingham is the second-largest port in the UK, and yet there are few ships, and we saw no seafarers. Ships come in and out on a single tide. No-one has time to get off.

Volvo, Saab and BMW import cars, but most of the traffic is in bulk fuel and iron ore, which involves very little labour. Three million tonnes of coal a year are imported through Immingham.

Hull's biggest private-sector employer is British Aerospace at Brough, where it builds Hawks for export to Indonesia.

164

In her biography of
Rimbaud, Enid Starkie
referred to an idea
that the mention of
Scarborough's Grand
Hotel in 'Promontoire',
in *Illuminations*, was the
result of a visit, but
Rimbaud could equally
have seen it in an
illustration. The Grand
Hotel would have been
only a few years old.

Michael Andrews's
painting *Lights VI: The Spa*
of 1974 is a similar view of
Scarborough's South Bay to
that at the top of page 169,
to which he added a
fictional six-lane coastal
highway crossing a large
suspension bridge.

The architecture of
St Mary's, Whitby, is
very unusual. The church
dates from 1110, but was
extended several times
after 1697 to accommodate
up to 2,000 people in box
pews and galleries, which
are reached by steps
outside. The interior is well
lit by skylights, installed in
1612, which resemble those
of a ship.

We visited Scarborough to confirm the details of Rimbaud's
Promontory Palace. Rimbaud was in Java in 1876.

In the afternoon, we sat on a bench outside St Mary's Church,
Whitby.

It is about a hundred years since the *Demeter* arrived in Whitby harbour. Its fifty 'great wooden boxes of earth' were consigned to Mr Samuel Billington, a Whitby solicitor, who had them sent on to Purfleet by train.

Captain James Cook began his career as ship's boy on the *Freelove*.

Dracula was published in 1897. The bench in the churchyard is first mentioned in chapter VI, which ends with the first sighting of the *Demeter*, a Russian schooner. The ship is driven into the harbour during a terrible storm, deserted but for the captain's corpse lashed to the helm and a huge dog which leaps ashore and disappears. The boxes are its only cargo.

Cook's ship *Endeavour* was a Whitby cat. Cats were built at Whitby for the coal trade with London: sturdy, spacious and flat-bottomed so they could be beached. Cook had worked on cats for nine years before joining the navy. He also chose them for his voyages to the Arctic and Antarctic.

On the evening of October 11th, we arrived in Redcar.

British Steel's plant at Redcar is one of four major steelworks in the country. It produces 70,000 tonnes of steel a week, 70 per cent of which is exported, much of it to the Far East, and employs hardly any people. The steel industry's current export surplus is about three-quarters of a billion pounds.

Wilton is one of the biggest chemical production sites in Europe. It produces about forty intermediate products. The chemical industry's export surplus is about £4 billion.

The service sector's share of exports has declined since 1960, as a result of the near-extinction of the merchant-shipping fleet.

The Tees is the UK's biggest single port. It imports iron ore and coal and exports oil and petroleum products.

In 1995, Chancellor of the Exchequer Kenneth Clarke told 250,000 listeners to a local radio interview: 'At Consett you have got one of the best steelworks in Europe. It doesn't employ as many people as it used to because it is so modern.' He meant the one at Redcar. Consett's steelworks closed in 1980 with the loss of 3,000 jobs. Kevin Earley, deputy leader of Derwentside District Council, said later: 'I was shocked to find Consett steelworks was still open. I went to my window and looked out, but I couldn't find it.' ¶

The traffic in the Tees estuary is largely bulk – imports of iron ore and coal for the steelworks at Redcar, exports of chemicals from the plants at Billingham and Wilton, and oil and petroleum products. The large volume of oil exported is the product of a Norwegian field in the North Sea, which comes ashore by pipeline. There is not much container or semi-bulk (timber etc.) traffic.

Unemployment in Middlesbrough is 17 per cent, the highest in the country, which has the least-regulated labour market in the industrialized world and the highest prison population of any nation in Europe.

We stopped to watch the Queen arrive at the Samsung site at Wynyard Park.

With £58 million of government aid, Samsung have invested £450 million in a plant which employs between 500 and 600 people producing microwave ovens and computer monitors. There was a small demonstration by the Committee to Defend Socialism in South Korea.

Wynyard Park is the estate of Sir John Hall, the developer of the Gateshead Metro Centre. He bought it in 1987 for £3 million from the Marquess of Londonderry, whose family were formerly coal-owners, and has developed golf-courses, housing estates and a hotel, which was *not* the one we stayed in.

As late as 1830, only 154 people lived in Middlesbrough, but in the next thirty years it grew faster than any other town in England. In 1995, despite its concentration of highly successful manufacturing industry and the Tees being the country's biggest port, Middlesbrough's unemployment was 17 per cent, the highest in the country. As in Liverpool, one might have thought that the decline of a town or city was a result of the collapse of its main industries, but the industries themselves are flourishing. The collapse is in the numbers of people they employ. ¶

Samsung's development was announced in December 1994, when Michael Heseltine estimated that it would employ 4,000 people. The site was opened by the Queen on October 13th 1995.

Sir John Hall was born in Ashington in 1933 and began his career as a mining surveyor with the National Coal Board, with which he qualified as a chartered surveyor. In 1969, he founded Cameron Hall Developments. The Metro Centre opened in 1985. He bought Wynyard Hall and the surrounding 7,500 acres in 1987 and was knighted in 1991. In 1992, having sold the Metro Centre to the Church Commissioners, he bought a controlling interest in Newcastle United Football Club.

Sterne was vicar of Sutton-on-the-Forest from 1738 until his death in 1768 and of Coxwold from 1760 to 1768. He lived at Shandy Hall from 1760 to 1768, when not abroad or in London. Shandy Hall is owned by the Laurence Sterne Trust; the house and garden are open to visitors.

In 1955, the Ministry of Defence purchased a 246-acre farm north of the A59, about ten kilometres west of Harrogate. In 1960, the US army security field station began operating there. In 1966, control was transferred to the US National Security Agency. The site was chosen because it is virtually free from electro-magnetic interference. By 1994, there were twenty-one radomes and a 32,000-line telephone connection from the nearby Hunter's Stone communications tower. Some 1,800 people worked at the base, 1,200 US Department of Defense personnel and 600 UK nationals, including, according to the MoD, a 'significant GCHQ presence'. For many years, there have been allegations that Menwith Hill allows the US to intercept commercial telecommunications in ways which may prejudice UK interests.

In the morning, we travelled south to Shandy Hall: 'Here dwelt Laurence Sterne, many years incumbent of Coxwold. Here he wrote *Tristram Shandy*, and *The Sentimental Journey*. Died in London in 1768.'

Near Harrogate, we passed the US National Security Agency's installation at Menwith Hill. This is the largest signals intelligence base in the world and eavesdrops on telephone and other communications, some of the most sensitive of which concern the exploitation of buckminster-fullerenes.

Robinson was beginning to act strangely.

As we came down from the Pennines, we passed Samlesbury, and he tried to get past the security.

In Preston, he went to another British Aerospace plant, but it had been demolished.

He kept trying to tell me about David Hart and his attempts to get the MoD to abandon the Tornado and lease second-hand F16s, about Gothic cathedrals, and that Hollywood had overtaken aerospace as the leading American export.

On the evening of October 23rd, he told me he was going out to steal a piece of equipment from one the Saudi Arabian Tornados.

The BAe site at Samlesbury was formerly the English Electric factory, where the Canberra and Lightning aircraft were built in the 1950s and '60s.

With the Eurofighter programme delayed almost ten years, Hart advocated leasing F16s from the USAF, rather than upgrading the Tornado F3, the option preferred by the RAF and Michael Heseltine. In March 1996, the MoD announced a £125-million upgrade for about a hundred Tornado F3s, to be carried out at Warton. By 1998, 120 Tornados had been supplied to Saudi Arabia.

In the early morning of January 29th 1996, Lotta Kronlid, Joanne Wilson, Andrea Needham and Angie Zelter, of the Ploughshares Movement, cut a hole in the fence at BAe's site at Warton. In full view of security cameras, they prised open the doors of a hangar and attacked a Hawk aircraft which was to have been delivered to Indonesia that year. The £500-million deal had been signed in 1993 in defiance of ten UN resolutions condemning Indonesian repression in East Timor, and involved a £65-million aid package to Indonesia to build the Samarinda power station in Kalimantan, displacing indigenous people and speeding the deforestation of one of South-east Asia's last remaining rain-forests. They punctured the fuselage and caused £1.5 million worth of damage to radar and missile-guidance systems.

Blackpool is Robinson's home-town. His parents used to have a nursery which specialized in strains of giant vegetables.

He explained that life on Earth evolved after the arrival of buckminsterfullerenes in meteorites.

He showed me where the Wellington bomber was built, with a geodetic structure invented by Barnes Wallis.

We arrived in Blackpool on the second day of Diwali, in the last week of the Illuminations.

Robinson says that Blackpool holds the key to his utopia . . .

W. Robinson & Sons' nursery at Forton, near Preston, is *The Home of the Mammoth Onion*.

In April 1996, the US journal *Science* published a confirmation that buckminsterfullerenes found in a meteor crater at Sudbury, Ontario, were extraterrestrial, supporting the idea that comets and meteorites bombarding the Earth helped create life by introducing vital organic compounds.

Vickers built Wellingtons at Squires Gate, which is now Blackpool Airport. Between 1940 and 1943, 1,653 were built there; the last Wellington was built at Squires Gate in 1945. The geodetic framework gave the aircraft its ability to keep flying even when heavily damaged. After the war, Hawker took over the factory and produced Hunter jet fighters.

Chamfort supported the Revolution, but in 1793 spoke out against violence. To escape prison, he tried to kill himself with a razor and a pistol, but managed only to inflict terrible wounds, from which he died five months later. The sentence is from *The Life of the Automobile* by Ilya Ehrenburg, translated by Joachim Neugroschel (London, 1985).

Designed by a landscape architect called Mawson, Stanley Park in Blackpool was opened by Baron Stanley of Preston, Earl of Derby, in 1926. It was Mawson who said: 'Blackpool stands between us and Revolution.' Le Corbusier's *Vers une architecture*, with its final chapter 'Architecture or Revolution', was published in 1923, though not in English translation until 1931.

The Trident submarine in the picture on page 195 is HMS *Vigilant*, which by April 1996 was at sea on contractor's trials. Of the four built, it was the third Trident to be completed. ¶

He often repeated Chamfort's favourite saying: 'In each man's life there comes the moment when his heart must either burst or turn to stone.'

'Blackpool stands between us and Revolution.'

Radiation levels in the Irish Sea are higher than in any other sea anywhere in the world . . .

We crossed the Irish Sea to Barrow, where the third Trident submarine was nearing completion.

Robinson said that he had to be in Newcastle by the end of the week. Then he said that he needed a day off to visit a relation.

BNFL's site at Drigg has been the national disposal site for low-level radioactive waste since the 1950s. It also stores plutonium-contaminated material (PCM). ¶

Nirex was set up in 1983 to look for sites for permanent disposal of up to 400,000 cubic metres of intermediate-level radioactive waste that were expected to have accumulated by 2060. Its application to excavate a 'rock characterization facility' was turned down in March 1977 following a public inquiry.

In its annual report in July 1997, the Radioactive Waste Advisory Committee stated that Nirex was the wrong body to deal with radioactive waste and urged the government to start again from scratch. ¶ ¶

The 190-tonne heat exchangers were taken to Drigg by road at night. The reactor core and pressure vessel were dismantled using a robotic arm and packed into 180 two-metre cubes for storage as intermediate-level waste.

The Thermal Oxide Reprocessing Plant (Thorp) at Sellafield was first proposed in the early 1970s. BNFL gained planning permission in 1978 after a long public inquiry. By August 1996, it had reprocessed only enough spent fuel to produce one tonne of plutonium. In July 1997, the plant was still unable to reach full production.

He took me to the dump at Drigg, where low-level radioactive waste is stored in deteriorating conditions, and to the site where Nirex were proposing to build an underground repository for intermediate-level waste.

At Sellafield, the 1963 reactor's heat exchangers were being removed as the first stage of dismantling the reactor. The Thorp reprocessing plant had finally started up in February 1995. Robinson said that it was unlikely ever to be even an *economic* proposition.

He told me that the plutonium aftermath of the nuclear industry will remain lethal for quarter of a million years.

At Wordsworth's birthplace, I thought he was going to go in and register a complaint . . .

On October 30th, without warning, we were told that our contracts had been terminated, and we heard on the car radio that a Tornado had crashed in the North Sea . . .

The great majority of published images of Hadrian's Wall are of the view looking east to Cuddy's Crag, near Housesteads fort. In an attempt to reduce the erosion caused by the large number of visitors to this site, the National Trust, as landowner, decided that it would no longer give permission for photography there. At the same time, British Telecom introduced a series of phonecards with images of sites managed by English Heritage, one of which was the view of Hadrian's Wall at Cuddy's Crag.

Prehistoric rock art is found in a number of localities in northern England and Scotland. The carvings were made between 3,000 and 2,000 BC, probably by semi-nomadic or migratory people who were animal herders, and are often found on rising ground overlooking panoramic views. The largest and most complex carvings are on horizontal surfaces of natural rock outcrops and on large boulders. Their meaning is thought to be both sacred and topographical and they incorporate motifs found elsewhere in the world. These motifs resemble entoptic forms characteristic of the early stages of trance experience.

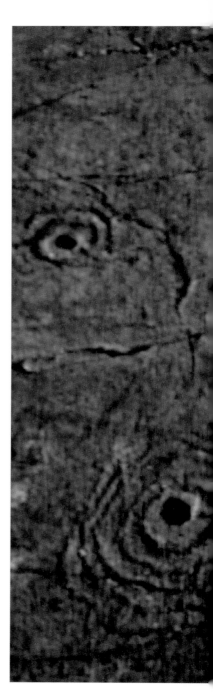

I cannot tell you where Robinson finally
found his utopia.

Further Notes

¶ page 2 Rimbaud left London on July 31st 1874 to take up a job teaching French. 165 King's Road, Reading, was then the address of Camille Le Clair, who had been advertising various courses in French at addresses in Reading since 1872. On July 25th, he had announced his move to 165 King's Road, then known as Montpellier House, in the *Reading Mercury*. The size of the house and the number of courses offered suggest that he employed several teachers. Rimbaud was not in Reading for long, and his advertisement does not seem to have been successful. By Christmas 1874, he was at his mother's in Charleville, and he never went back to England. See Enid Starkie, *Arthur Rimbaud* (London, 1961).

In 1995, 165 and 167 King's Road, Reading, were the empty shells of a pair of large semidetached houses awaiting reconstruction by the Wiltshier construction company. Known together as Palladio House, they seem to have been called this before they were gutted. The image at the bottom of page 3 was photographed on March 28th 1995, the first day of photography for the film *Robinson in Space*.

¶¶ page 2 In his *Postmodern Geographies* (London, 1989), Edward Soja quotes John Berger:

'We hear a lot about the crisis of the modern novel. What this involves, fundamentally, is a change in the mode of narration. It is scarcely any longer possible to tell a straight story sequentially unfolding in time. And this is because we are too aware of what is continually traversing the story-line laterally. That is to say, instead of being aware of a point as an infinitely small part of a straight line, we are aware of it as an infinitely small part of an infinite number of lines, as the centre of a star of lines. Such awareness is the result of our constantly having to take into account the simultaneity and extension of events and possibilities.

'There are many reasons why this should be so: the range of modern means of communication: the scale of modern power: the degree of personal political responsibility that must be accepted for events all over the world: the fact that the world has become indivisible: the unevenness of economic development within that world: the scale of the exploitation. All these play a part. Prophecy now involves a geographical rather than historical projection; it is space, not time, that hides consequences from us. To prophesy today it is only necessary to know men as they are throughout the world in all their inequality. Any contemporary narrative which ignores the urgency of this dimension is incomplete and acquires the oversimplified character of a fable' (p. 22).

For Nietzsche in Turin, see *Selected Letters of Friedrich Nietzsche*, edited and translated by Christopher Middleton (Chicago, 1969).

¶ page 5 The first Sherlock Holmes story is *A Study in Scarlet*, which begins:

'In the year 1878 I took my degree of Doctor of Medicine of the University of London, and proceeded to Netley to go through the course prescribed for surgeons in the Army. Having completed my studies there, I was duly attached to the Fifth Northumberland Fusiliers as assistant surgeon. The regiment was stationed in India at the time, and before I could join it, the second Afghan war had broken out.'

Watson joins his regiment at Kandahar:

'The campaign brought honours and promotion to many, but for me it had nothing but misfortune and disaster. I was removed from my brigade and attached to the Berkshires, with whom I served at the fatal battle of Maiwand. There I was struck on the shoulder by a Jezail bullet, which shattered the bone and grazed the subclavian artery. I should have fallen into the hands of the murderous Ghazis had it not been for the devotion and courage shown by Murray, my orderly, who threw me across a pack-horse, and succeeded in bringing me safely to the British lines.'

Watson is sent home to convalesce. In the Criterion Bar, he is tapped on the shoulder by 'young Stamford, who had been a dresser under me at Bart's'. Stamford introduces him to Holmes, who is seeking someone to share rooms in Baker Street.

¶¶ page 5 The passage from which it comes is as follows:

'The idea of a new life is at once realistic and illusory – and hence neither true nor false. What is true is that the preconditions for a different life have already been created, and that that other life is thus on the cards. What is false is the assumption that being on the cards and being imminent are the same thing, that what is immediately possible is necessarily a world away from what is only a distant possibility, or even an impossibility. The fact is that the space which contains the realized preconditions of another life is the same one as prohibits what those preconditions make possible. The seeming limpidity of that space is therefore a delusion: it appears to make elucidation unnecessary, but in reality it urgently requires elucidation. A total revolution – material, economic, social, political, psychic, cultural, erotic, etc. – seems to be in the offing, as though already immanent to the present. To change life, however, we must first change space.'

206

¶ page 6 Later buses seem to reflect a decline in the status of public transport, and of the public realm generally – the stress and delays of one-person-operation; lurches from failing automatic gearboxes and poor suspension; interiors clumsily assembled from aluminium extrusions and flat sheets; and doors to prevent informal entry and exit. At the price of a tacky refurbishment by one of the present-day manufacturers, about a thousand Routemasters remain in London, some on routes now handed over to private contractors, and they have outlasted many of their successors. Others have been sold to China, Sri Lanka and post-deregulation operators in other UK towns and cities, including Reading.

Reading Mainline was set up by Mike Russell, a former employee of Reading Transport, the municipal bus company. Mainline's driver-and-conductor service is quicker than that of the modern, one-person-operated buses, and they expanded their fleet from eighteen to forty-four, including twelve which had previously been in service on the Blackpool promenade. On June 1st 1998, Reading Mainline was bought by Reading Transport with a commitment to continue to run at least twenty Routemasters for at least two years.

¶¶ page 6 In September 1994, the French Institute of International Relations published a report on Britain and its institutions which placed the social disintegration characteristic of the Tory years in a context of decline dating from 1945, when the UK failed to take the lead in Europe. Fabrice Rousselot, at the time UK correspondent for *Libération,* commented: '. . . as regards the economy . . . Britain always seems to swing between boom and bust. It's because you have no real manufacturing base any more. Everything has to be imported.'

Elwes's study was picked up by BBC2's *Money Programme* a couple of weeks after the 1997 General Election. The programme commissioned the consultants Wolff Olins to propose various rebranding exercises including a redesign of the Union flag that somewhat anticipated the paint job carried out by British Airways on their aircraft later in the year. After the election, the rebranding of 'Britain' as a 'young country' was vigorously pursued by the Blair government with the assistance of the think-tank Demos. In all these projects, a social critique seems to overlap with a perception of failure in manufacturing and design; like Fabrice Rousselot, Demos equate Euroscepticism with the UK's reputation for producing overpriced, ugly, low-technology products.

¶¶ page 11 The Duke of Cumberland took over command of the army, but Hawley retained command of the cavalry. Cumberland's reputation as the 'Butcher' of Culloden is probably due at least partly to Hawley's excesses. James Wolfe, who had been his brigade-major at Falkirk, wrote: 'They could not make choice of a more unsuitable person, for the troops dread his severity, hate the man, and hold his military knowledge in contempt.' In 1752, he became governor of Portsmouth. He died in 1759, leaving his house to his adopted son, who was almost certainly his illegitimate child by his housekeeper, a Mrs Toovey.

The house at West Green was rebuilt in its present form by Hawley in the mid-eighteenth century. On the garden façade, there are panels containing four busts of Roman emperors and another of Bacchus. Over the door is the inscription *Fay ce que vouldras* (Do as you will), the quotation from Rabelais (*Gargantua*, chap. 57) which was the motto of Sir Francis Dashwood's Hell-Fire Club, inscribed above the entrance to its meeting place at Medmenham Abbey and over the fireplaces there. Dashwood had developed a fervent antipathy to the Roman Catholic Church during visits to Italy and founded the Dilettanti Society in 1733. In 1745, George Bubb Dodington, Lord Melcombe Regis, wrote to him: '. . . we are all in love with your agreeable Defence of that Steady Course you are in, of employing 20 of the 24 hours either upon your own Belly, or from thence, like a Publick Reservoir, administering to those of other People, by laying your Cock in every private Family that has any Place fitt to receive it.' According to the present Sir Francis Dashwood, the Hell-Fire Club was probably started as early as the 1740s, so Hawley may have been a visitor to Medmenham or one of its predecessors, or he may merely have adopted the same motto. Rabelais apparently adopted it from St Augustine, who when asked, 'What must I do to be saved?' replied: 'Love God and do what you like.' Most of this is from *Country Life* (November 21st 1936) and the booklet *West Wycombe Caves* by Sir Francis Dashwood, Bt.

West Green House remained in the ownership of Hawley's descendants until 1874. In 1904, it was bought by Evelyn, Duchess of Wellington, widow of the third Duke; it was given to the National Trust by the Sassoon family in 1956. Alistair, later Lord, McAlpine was the Trust's tenant from 1973 until 1990 and is reported to have spent more than £50,000 a year in renovations, decorations and development of the garden. McAlpine became Margaret Thatcher's party treasurer, aged thirty-two, in 1975, 'a toad turned into a prince by her kiss' (Julian Critchley). In 1979, he was made deputy chairman as well. At Christmas, he was usually Thatcher's house guest at Chequers. He had previously been best known as an art collector, and for his enthusiasm for exotic animals.

The gate-posts and obelisk were designed by Terry in 1975. Terry was also commissioned to design a triumphal arch to celebrate Mrs Thatcher's election victory in 1979, but it was not built. West Green House was badly damaged by fire during McAlpine's tenancy and was bombed by the IRA shortly after he left. The sale of its contents raised over £1.7 million, of which £250,000 was for the wine cellar. Thatcher described McAlpine as 'one of the most effective fund-raisers of all time, and one of my closest and most loyal friends'.

After her deposition, he became increasingly critical of the Conservatives.

¶ page 40 The ten major world ports in 1994 were: Rotterdam, 294 million tonnes; Singapore, 224 million tonnes; Shanghai, 166 million tonnes; Hong Kong, 111 million tonnes; Nagoya, 120 million tonnes; Antwerp, 110 million tonnes; Yokohama, 103 million tonnes; Marseilles, 91 million tonnes; Long Beach, 88 million tonnes; Pusan, 82 million tonnes.

The eleven largest ports in the UK in 1994 were: London, 52 million tonnes; Forth, 44 million tonnes; Tees & Hartlepool, 43 million tonnes; Grimsby & Immingham, 42.9 million tonnes; Sullum Voe, 39 million tonnes; Milford Haven, 34 million tonnes; Southampton, 32 million tonnes; Liverpool, 29 million tonnes; Felixstowe, 22 million tonnes; Medway, 15 million tonnes; Dover, 14 million tonnes.

UK ports with the largest foreign, non-oil traffic in 1994 were: Felixstowe, 22 million tonnes; Grimsby & Immingham, 21 million tonnes; Tees & Hartlepool, 17 million tonnes; London, 16 million tonnes; Dover, 14 million tonnes; Port Talbot, 11 million tonnes; Liverpool, 10 million tonnes; Hull, 9 million tonnes; Medway, 7 million tonnes.

The port of 'London' consists of the Port of London Authority's entire jurisdiction from Teddington Lock to Foulness, the Thames estuary over more than 100 kilometres. The largest single location of port activity is at Tilbury, where the docks are now owned by Forth Ports plc, but with a total traffic of only 7 million tonnes (1994) Tilbury itself is not a large port. A lot of the traffic in the Thames is to and from other UK ports, especially that in oil. The Humber now has more *foreign* traffic than the Thames estuary: in 1994, the combined total in foreign traffic for London and the Medway (which is a separate entity) was 39 million tonnes, compared with a combined total of 52 million tonnes at the Humber ports of Grimsby & Immingham, Hull, Goole and the rivers Trent, Ouse and Humber. London's *foreign, non-oil* traffic was only 16 million tonnes.

The Forth, with the second-largest traffic, is as fragmented as the Thames; 40 million tonnes of this was oil. Next were the port authorities of Tees & Hartlepool, and Grimsby & Immingham, with about 43 million tonnes each. The fifth- and sixth-largest totals were at Sullum Voe, an oil terminal in the Shetlands, with 39 million tonnes, almost entirely outgoing crude oil, and Milford Haven, with 34 million tonnes, again almost all oil. Southampton and Liverpool, being neither fragmented nor specialized, could be described as the UK's largest 'conventional' ports. The other two big ports in the UK are Felixstowe, which had the largest foreign, non-oil traffic and which handles 40 per cent of *all* the UK's container traffic, and Dover, which, despite the Channel Tunnel, still handles 50 per cent of international roll-on roll-off traffic.

It is presumably a mistake to assess a port's importance solely on the basis of the tonnage of its traffic. Container and road-vehicle loads probably represent considerably greater monetary value than bulk materials. On this basis, Felixstowe probably handles the traffic with the greatest value.

¶ page48 Sheerness is the main port of the Medway. It is the largest vehicle-handling port in the UK. Medway Ports was privatized in 1989 as a management-employee buy-out and was sold in October 1993 to the Mersey Docks and Harbour Company for £100 million, a transaction which made Medway's former chief executive a multi-millionaire three months after he bought 100,000 shares from other Medway directors. Medway had previously sacked 300 dockers for refusing to accept new contracts. On dismissal, the dockers were obliged to surrender their shares in the company at a valuation of £2.50 per share, shortly before MDHC bought them for £37.25 each.

¶ page 56 Sir Alec Issigonis was born in Turkey. The family emigrated to England, where his parents wanted him to become an artist, but he studied engineering. He worked for Humber in Coventry before joining Morris Motors in Oxford in 1936. During the war, he designed the Morris Minor. In 1945, the Labour government asked the car industry to produce a cheap, robust car in large numbers. Rootes were offered the Volkswagen, but turned it down. William Morris, Lord Nuffield, had dismissed Issigonis's car as a 'poached egg', but it was put into production in 1948. It was a successful, innovative design which sold well and made money: one million cars were built in the first eleven years of production, which continued until 1972. Many of the cars survive today. It is often suggested that if the company had put any effort into exporting it, the Minor could have been at least as successful as the more complicated Volkswagen as a 'world car'. Issigonis's Mini was launched in 1959 and was still in production in 1998. It was the first car with the transverse engine, front-wheel drive and space-efficient concept which are now the global standard for small- and medium-sized cars. By the mid-1960s, Issigonis had reinvented the European small car and provided BMC with at least two world-beating designs, but the company again failed to take the initiative, partly because, with the UK still outside the EC, volume exports to the main European markets were blocked by tariffs. With a restricted market, the company was unprofitable, and after 1968 its situation deteriorated under a succession of design-blind managers, most of whom lacked experience of the car industry and squandered Issigonis's legacy (see Karel Williams *et al.*, *Cars: Analysis, History, Cases* [Providence, 1994]).

Until 1992, British Aerospace had been attempting to diversify away from aircraft production since the mid-1980s. Its purchases of Royal Ordnance and Rover from the government included large land holdings; it owns construction and property companies and was co-owner, with Hutchison Whampoa, of the Orange mobile telephone network until the latter's flotation.

The property company Arlington was bought by BAe in 1989 to develop land owned by Rover and Royal Ordnance. The demolition of much of the factory at Cowley took place before the sale to BMW, and by March 1998 Arlington had developed a retail park with a Tesco superstore and various other sheds, and a business park with a Whitbread Beefeater theme pub and Travel Inn, a large Royal Mail depot and a number of office buildings. More office buildings were under construction, including one for the Inland Revenue, but much of the site was still vacant.

¶ page 67 It is certainly easy to find a disconcerting aesthetic in the post-Conservative landscape, especially in the country. The windowless sheds of the *logistics* industry, road construction, spiky mobile phone aerials, a proliferation of new fencing of various types, security guards, police helicopters and cameras, new prisons, agribusiness, UK and US military bases, mysterious research and training centres, 'independent' schools, eerie commuter villages, rural poverty and the country houses of rich and powerful men of unrestrained habits are visible features of a landscape in which the suggestion of *cruelty* is never very far away.

In their book *Too Close to Call* (London, 1995), Sarah Hogg and Jonathan Hill describe the strategy behind the 1992 Conservative election campaign: 'Throughout the summer [1991], Saatchi's had been refining their thinking. Maurice Saatchi's thesis went like this. In retrospect at least, 1979, 1983 and 1987 appeared to be very simple elections to win. The choice was clear: "efficient but cruel" Tories versus "caring but incompetent" Labour. The difficulty for the Conservatives in 1991 was that the recession had killed the "efficient" tag – leaving only the "cruel". While the Tory party had successfully blunted the "cruel" image by replacing Margaret Thatcher with some-one seen as more "caring", Maurice did not believe that John Major should fight the election on soft "caring" issues.'

In the subsequent period, the Conservatives were seen as even less efficient and even more cruel. The shackling of women prisoners during labour, and its defence by Ann Widdecombe, the Home Office minister, was the most outrageous example of this, but the campaign to legitimize child-beating was perhaps more shocking because it was so widespread. The sexuality of Conservatism is certainly very strange. While there are always a few straightforward libertines among prominent Tories, and Thatcher apparently tolerated homosexuals when it suited her, repression and S&M haunt the Conservatives in a way which cannot be put down simply to the influence of public schools. Like repression, the unregulated market inflicts pain and suffering. Unemployment, increased inequality, low

211

wages and longer working hours all lead to depression, ill health and shorter life expectancy. In May 1996, Maurice Saatchi launched another pre-election campaign with the slogan: 'Yes it hurt. Yes it worked.'

¶ page 93 On one of the gates, below a large arrow pointing to the right, is the inscription: *This Road from Wimborne to Dorchester was projected and completed through the instrumentality of J S W SAWBRIDGE ERLE DRAX Esq. M.P. in the Years 1841 and 1842.* As Pevsner's *Buildings of England* (Harmondsworth, 1972) puts it, '. . .he succeeded in getting the main Wimborne to Dorchester road re-routed to give him a much enlarged park.'

Most of the following derives from an 1870 *History of Dorset*: The Erle family acquired the Charborough estate by marriage in the mid-sixteenthth century. In the Civil War, Sir Walter Erle was the commander of the Parliamentary force which beseiged Corfe Castle, and Charborough House was burnt down by Royalist troops. The present house dates from the rebuilding in about 1660. At the death of Sir Walter, the estate was inherited by his grandson, who died in 1720, leaving an only daughter, Frances, who married Sir Edward Ernley, MP for Wareham, and died in 1728, also leaving an only daughter, Elizabeth, who married Henry Drax of Ellerton Abbey, Yorkshire, near the village of Drax.

In 1647, as a defeated Royalist, Lieutenant-Colonel James Drax sold his estate in Yorkshire and settled, as did other Royalist families, in Barbados, which was not then under Parliamentary rule and where the sugar boom had begun. Having made a fortune in slave-worked sugar, he married the daughter of the Earl of Carlisle, who was the 'proprietor' of the island. In the 'rebellion' of 1650, Drax supported the governor and was for a time imprisoned by the rebels on his estate.

The Drax fortune seems to have survived various reversals. Drax Hall, probably built in the 1650s, is one of the earliest and biggest sugar properties in Barbados and the oldest surviving Jacobean mansion in the western hemisphere. In *The Slave Trade* (London, 1997), Hugh Thomas writes: '. . .the planters who carried out the sugar revolution, such as James Drax, eventually went home to England as rich men, and their families began to think of their Caribbean sugar properties as if they were gold mines.' In 1870, the family still retained an estate at Carlisle Bay, Barbados.

In 1692, the estate of Henry Drax was vested by an act of Parliament in Thomas Shatterden, gent. His son Henry assumed the name and arms of Drax and married Elizabeth Ernley, inheriting the estates of both Ernley and Erle. In 1870, the only portrait in the house of anyone not a member of the family was of Lieutenant-General Henry Hawley of West Green. The present owner of Charborough has abandoned multiple names and calls himself simply Mr H. W. Drax.

212

The village of Drax in Yorkshire gives its name to the largest power station in the country.

¶ page 130 In the 1994 edition of *Port Statistics*, based on figures for the twelve months of 1993, the Mersey Dock and Harbour Company's operating profit was just under £21 million. The MDHC bought the profitable Medway Ports in October 1993 and operate a ferry service and container terminal in Northern Ireland, but during 1993 Liverpool nonetheless seemed to be 'the most profitable port in the UK'. With larger UK ports fragmented or specialized, Liverpool can also be described as 'the UK's largest conventional port'. In September 1995, when the photographs in this book were taken, Liverpool's port traffic was greater than at any time in its history.

This commercial success belies the spectacular dereliction of the waterfronts of Liverpool and Birkenhead. While it may appear that this dereliction is a symptom of a decline in their traffic, and that Liverpool's impoverishment is a result of this decline, it is nothing of the kind. If Liverpool as a city is not what it was a hundred years ago, this is not because its port traffic has declined, but because, like so much other economic activity, a port does not occupy space in the way that it used to.

What has vanished from Liverpool is not the working port itself, but the contribution which it made to the city's economy. A large proportion of the dock traffic is now in containers and bulk, both of which are highly automated and pass through Liverpool without generating many ancillary jobs. With the direct rail link to Europe, these ancillary jobs may even be outside the UK. Also, like any English city outside London, Liverpool is now largely a branch-office location, having long ago lost the headquarters (White Star, Cunard) which made it a world city, the point of departure for emigrants from all over Europe to the New World.

Liverpool has also been transformed by the virtual elimination of the UK's merchant-shipping fleet. Most of the few remaining British seafarers work on car, passenger or freight ferries, on which the majority of jobs are in catering. Apart from the decline in UK-owned ships and UK crews, modern merchant ships are very large and very sparsely crewed; there are never many ships in even a large modern port, they don't stay long, and crews have little – if any – time ashore, assuming they have money to spend.

The warehouses which used to line both sides of the Mersey have been superseded by a fragmented and mobile space: vehicles moving or parked on the UK's roads, which serve as a publicly funded warehouse. This is most visible on summer evenings, when busy trunk roads on which parking is permitted become truck dormitories. Many of these trucks are bound for the enormous warehouses of inland distribution estates near motorway junctions – Wakefield 41, for example, at junction 41 of the M1, just south of its junction with the M62. The road haulage – or *logistics* – industry does not typically base its depots in port cities, but it is intimately linked to them. With long distances travelled, and lightweight buildings with artificially maintained interior environments, the insubstantiality of the modern industrial landscape seems to be achieved only at the expense of very high levels of energy consumption.

Despite having shed the majority of its workforce, the Liverpool port's attitude to its remaining dockers has been extremely aggressive. In September 1995, two weeks after telling *Lloyd's List* that it had the most productive workforce in Europe, the MDHC's sacking of 329 of its 500 remaining dockers was triggered by their refusal to cross a picket line in support of fellow employees of a contract labour firm. The subsequent strike attracted international support. On January 26th 1998, the dockers voted to accept the MDHC's offer of a £28,000 pay-off for each worker and ended the dispute. It seemed that, for the company, the issue was not money or specific working practices, but a concerted attempt to rid the port of any memory of its culture and traditions. As at the new Thamesport container terminal on the Medway, which its management says is 'not a port', these are seen as impediments to development and, unlike the physical structures on the waterfront, have been cleared away.

¶ page 135   Wherever one went, one could rely on the rooms being almost exactly the same. Naturally, they were nearly always full, but one learnt to book ahead, and there were more Travel Inns opening every week. The Travel Inn made it possible to travel around the UK in a way which was not really possible before, when staying with friends – like some latter-day Celia Fiennes – was the only way to avoid the psychological difficulties involved in staying in the typical English 'hotel'. There were drawbacks – each Inn was paired with a theme pub or restaurant, usually a Beefeater or a Brewers Fayre, and sometimes a TGI Friday, but one could avoid these until breakfast, when miraculously they never smelled of last night's cigarette smoke. In the newer Inns, the bathroom sometimes had a slight smell of what was probably floor adhesive, but could be mistaken for an alcoholic odour sometimes found in derelict houses. The smell seemed to increase with ventilation, which was odd.

The equally priced Forte Travelodge generally smelled of air freshener and had the charm of being slightly dated, but these were always paired with a Little Chef or, if one was lucky, a Happy Eater. The Happy Eater was being phased out, possibly more because of its connections with ecstasy than with John Major. The Travel Inn breakfast was a little more generous, and they were never on a motorway, but usually within about 200 metres of a junction. The other competitor was a Granada Lodge, the least attractive option

214

and, at £39.95, overpriced. The only one we stayed in, at the Dartford Tunnel, was even more – £46.95 – and the rooms were small. According to Granada's list, the Exeter and Heathrow Lodges were also more expensive, but the Lodge at Grantham was only £27.95. In November 1995, Granada's Gerry Robinson launched his bid for Forte, asserting that Forte's were 'tired brands' and underpriced. Forte countered with a proposal to sell the Little Chef and Travelodge chains to Whitbread, but Granada raised its bid and took control of Forte on January 23rd 1996. Prices have since crept up and a Travel Inn cost £38 in early 1998, apart from three in central London. Robinson became chief executive of Granada in 1991, and in 1998 was also chairman of BSkyB, in which Granada has a stake. In 1992, he faced protests when David Plowright resigned as chairman of Granada Television over Robinson's cost-cutting. John Cleese sent him a fax which read: 'Why don't you fuck off out of it, you ignorant upstart caterer?' In January 1998, Gerry Robinson was appointed chairman of the Arts Council of England.

Our addiction to budget hotel chains was eventually cured in November 1995 by a week in the *Tankerville Arms*, in Wooler, Northumberland, which was both the cheapest and the best hotel encountered in seven months travelling in England.

¶¶ page 135   When the *Rocket* approached to pass by on the other track, Huskisson was returning to greet the Duke of Wellington, who had not alighted. The engineer of the *Rocket* tried to stop and called to Huskisson to get out of the way, but, bewildered by poor health, he remained standing by the open door, which was struck by the engine. It was not clear whether he was knocked down by the door or the engine itself, but he fell to the ground across one of the rails. The engine's wheels ran over his thigh and leg, and he died at nine o'clock that night. For a more detailed account, see Humphrey Jennings, *Pandaemonium*, edited by Mary-Lou Jennings and Charles Madge (London, 1985), which includes *174 – Opening of the Railway, September 15, 1830*, from *Mechanics' Magazine* (September 25th 1830).

¶ page 142   John Milne (1850–1913) grew up in Rochdale and was a pupil at Liverpool Collegiate School, where he won several prizes, one a book about Iceland. He was fascinated by geology and, having saved money secretly, he set out to go there. He studied at King's College, London, and the Royal School of Mines and, after experience in the mines of Lancashire and Cornwall and several expeditions, was invited to become a professor in Tokyo in 1875. In 1880, there was a disastrous earthquake which damaged much of the area around Tokyo and Yokohama. Milne called a public meeting, out of which the Seismological Society of Japan was established. During his time in Japan, he contributed over three-quarters of its journal, including articles on aspects of the earthquake from mythology and the texts of ancient scientists to accounts of small earthquakes he produced himself by dropping heavy weights or setting off large amounts of explosives. With Thomas Gray, he developed the Gray Milne Seismograph, which was superseded by his Milne Horizontal Pendulum Seismograph and later Milne-Shaw models developed with another colleague. By his thirty-seventh birthday, Milne had become a Fellow of the Royal Society, and in 1888 he received the Order of the Rising Sun from the Emperor of Japan. Before returning to England, he married Tone Horikawa, the daughter of the abbot of Gonjo-Ji, Hakidote, and they lived together at Shide, on the Isle of Wight, where his observatory became world-famous. His best-known books are *Earthquakes and Other Earth Movements* and *Seismology* (see Leslie Herbert-Gustar and Patrick A. Nett, *Professor John Milne FRS FGS 1850–1913, Biographical Notes* [Newport, Isle of Wight, 1973]).

¶¶ page 142   In July, supplies to 24,000 homes in Halifax were cut off for twenty-four hours as temperatures soared to thirty degrees C. A hosepipe ban had been in force for the previous three weeks in Halifax, Bradford and part of Leeds. The company appointed a public relations executive at a salary of £80,000 a year. In August, Yorkshire Water applied for drought orders to enable it to curtail water use and pump water out of the River Wharfe. At a public inquiry the following March, it was revealed that the mass evacuation of over a million people had been considered. In September, Sir Gordon Jones, the £189,000-a-year chairman of Yorkshire Water, was summoned to London to be questioned by ministers, while the company was preparing an emergency rota to cut off some consumers on alternate days and negotiating with soft-drinks companies to supply Halifax and Bradford with bottled tap water. Rain fell heavily in parts of Yorkshire during September, but 'in the wrong place'. The company's managing director said: 'I have not had a bath or shower for three months and nobody has noticed. You can wash adequately in half a bowl of water', but later admitted that he had taken baths in relatives' homes outside Yorkshire. It was reported that Yorkshire Water had applied for a government 'Chartermark' for high public-service standards. On November 14th, as a public inquiry opened at Dewsbury town hall, BBC Radio news reported 1,000 tankers in use in West Yorkshire, with parking on the hard shoulder of the M62. On November 27th, an emergency network of pipes and pumping stations was announced after confirmation that there was no hope of reservoirs filling in time to avert a second crisis the following summer, and half-yearly results showed increased profits despite the huge cost of the drought. On January 9th 1996, the threat of rota cuts was lifted, the drought orders were withdrawn, and the last 110-lorry road-tankering operation to Huddersfield was called off. Two weeks of rain had taken all the county's reservoirs over the 20-per-cent mark for the first time since August.

¶ page 155   In December 1995, Doncaster Prison was reported as having the highest rate of suicides and assaults of any prison in the country.

Out of 600 staff, 127 had resigned in the eighteen months since the prison had opened, and there was serious indiscipline amongst prisoners. The high-technology and camera-security regime, with a low staff-to-prisoner ratio, had ceased to be the cheapest in the country. Wackenhut had been investigated in the US for alleged financial irregularities.

In December 1995, Doncaster's International Railport began regular freight services with kilometre-long trains designed for direct connection with Europe through the Channel Tunnel. The first train carried steel, chemicals, engineering parts and foodstuffs, and travelled via Harwich to Zeebrugge, where it was split into separate services for Italy, Germany and Spain. It was hoped that the link would take 100,000 truck journeys off the UK's roads in the following year.

¶ page 157 The sale of British Coal's surviving pits to the private sector took effect on December 30th 1994. Richard Budge's RJB Mining bought seventeen pits for £815 million and leased a further three. The previous fifteen years had seen the closure of 200 pits and the loss of 200,000 miners' jobs. By April 1996, RJB's output was cheaper than Colombian coal, and the volume of imported coal had decreased. In the period 1991–8, the cost of UK deep-mined coal was reduced by 52 per cent. Although the coal unions regarded RJB as the safest private employer, in 1995–6 the rate of major injuries in its pits was 52 per cent higher than in 1994–5. When RJB's contracts with the electricity generators expired in 1998, the pits were facing competition from increasing numbers of open-cast sites, though there were hopes that the government's energy review would guarantee deep-mined production of 25 million tonnes a year.

For the story of MI5's campaigns against the NUM, see Seumas Milne, *The Enemy Within – The Secret War against the Miners* (London, 1995).

In 1984, David Hart obtained press accreditation and toured mining areas in a chauffeur-driven Mercedes, organizing disaffected miners. He was a main mover behind legal actions against the NUM which led to sequestration and receivership, and his interventions led to the creation of the breakaway UDM union. In the five years after the strike ended, he made over £1 million from property deals involving British Coal's pension funds. In October 1995, there was uproar in the House of Commons when Michael Portillo disclosed that Hart had been given top-level security clearance allowing him access to defence secrets submitted by British companies. A property dealer, he was discharged from bankruptcy in 1978. He inherited a fortune from his father, a founder of Ansbacher's merchant bank. After the miners' strike, he set up the Committee for a Free Britain and financed a newsletter, *British Briefing*, edited by a former MI5 officer in charge of 'counter-subversion', which attempted to smear Labour MP's as Communist sympathizers. As well as Portillo, he was said to include Peter Lilley and Malcolm Rifkind – who initiated his role at the Ministry of Defence – amongst his family friends. The late William Casey, head of the CIA under Ronald Reagan, was also a friend.

¶¶ page 157 Ian Fleming probably knew the name Drax from Jamaica, where in the late seventeenth century William Drax established a 3,000-acre pimento and sugar plantation at St Ann's Bay, which he named the Drax Hall Estate.

¶ page 161 The crew of the Arctic trawler *Lord Mountevans* may have provided the first reports of the convoy which carried missiles to Cuba in 1962. A Commander Brooks ran the operation from an office in the basement of a fishing company in the docks until it came to an abrupt end in the mid-1970s, prompting speculation that he may have been aboard the Hull trawler *Gaul*, which disappeared in February 1974 off the North Cape of Norway, and that the *Gaul* may have been stopped by the Soviet navy. Intelligence officers were carried by agreement with the owners, but without seeking the consent of the crews. Former Hull trawlermen have sought recognition of the surveillance work they carried out for the Royal Navy, which was ignored when the fishing fleet was run down following the 'cod war' with Iceland. The trawler owners were compensated, but crews were told that as casual workers they were not entitled to anything.

¶¶ page 161 Of William III, the *Dictionary of National Biography* offers: 'A quite unwarrantable interpretation, gravely accepted by so calm an historian as Lord Stanhope, has been put upon Burnet's awkward statement that "he had no vice but of one sort, in which he was very cautious and secret"'. This is a reference to William's relationships with William Bentinck, who became 1st Earl of Portland, and Arnoud van Keppel, created Earl of Albemarle in 1696. Bentinck's family were aristocrats in Holland, and he had been William's closest confidant since the 1670s. When the younger, handsome van Keppel became the King's favourite, Portland became very jealous, resigning in 1699. There was a deathbed reconciliation. William's affair with Betty, Elizabeth Villiers, a Lady of the Court, began in 1685 and lasted until Queen Mary's death in 1695, after which she married George Hamilton, who was made Earl of Orkney.

¶ page 173 In 1997, British Steel was the third-largest steel producer in the world, after Nippon (Japan) and Pohang (South Korea). In 1995, the UK produced 17.6 million tonnes of crude steel, of which 8.4 million tonnes were exported, and imported 5.7 million tonnes, a domestic consumption of 14.9 million tonnes. Exports were 4.5 million tonnes to the EU, 1 million to the rest of Europe, 1.4 million to Asia, 1.2 million to North America, 143,000 to Africa and 100,000 to South America. In 1970, the UK had produced 28.3 million tonnes of crude steel, of which 3.8 million tonnes were exported, and had imported 2.2 million tonnes, a domestic consumption of 26.7 million tonnes.

218

In 1993, ICI sold its nylon and polyester plants at Wilton to Du Pont, followed by polypropylene, to BASF, and ethylene oxide (for detergents, paints etc.) to Union Carbide, both in 1994. ICI bought Du Pont's acrylics business in the US. On October 9th 1995, there was a fire in a BASF warehouse containing 10,000 tonnes of polypropylene chips, which are used to make car bumpers and crisp packets. In July 1997, ICI was reported to be planning to sell most of the rest of Wilton to Du Pont, having bought Unilever's speciality chemicals division two months before, but by 1998 the only other sale was of a polythene plant to BP. In 1998, about 7,000 people were working at Wilton, 4,000 for ICI and 3,000 for other companies. ICI employ about 5,000 people on Teesside.

¶ page 179 In the 1980s, there were attempts to assert that the future for the UK's economy lay in services, and that the imbalance in imports of manufactured goods which characterized the Thatcher years could be sustained through increased exports of services, particularly of 'financial services'. Since the 1960s, much of the UK's manufacturing industry has disappeared, and the proportion of the workforce employed in the service industry has risen, but three-quarters of all employment is still manufacturing-related, and manufactured exports still sustain the balance of trade. In fact, because of the virtual disappearance of the merchant-shipping fleet, the service sector's share of exports has actually declined since 1960, and imports of cars, electronics and other *visible* items are balanced by exports not of services, but of *less visible* manufactured items, in particular intermediate products (for example, chemicals) and capital goods (power stations, airports, weapons). These strengths seem to match the financial sector's cultural preferences: chemical plants are capital-intensive, but do not involve the risks and ephemerality of product design; exports of capital goods are largely financed by other people's capital. The UK is good at low-investment, craft-based high technology, but not at high-investment, mass-produced high technology, unless it is owned and financed elsewhere (the US, Japan, South Korea or Germany). The UK's most extensive indigenous high-technology industry is weaponry, in which investment has been supported by the state. The UK's production of *desirable* artefacts is certainly lamentable (and confirms the stereotype of a nation run by philistines with unattractive attitudes to sex), but any perception of the demise of manufacturing industry based on its failure to produce technologically sophisticated, attractive consumer goods is bound to be overstated. Most UK manufacturing is unglamorous – intermediate products and capital goods are not branded items visible in the shops. Intermediate products, in particular, are often produced in *out-of-the-way* places like Sheerness or Immingham – places at the ends of roads. The UK's *domestically owned* manufacturing sector is now small, but its most successful concerns are efficient, highly automated and employ only a few people, many of whom are highly specialized technicians. The UK's *foreign-owned* manufacturing sector employs comparatively larger numbers of people in the production of cars, electronic products or components and other visible but internationally branded items. The big export earners in manufacturing, like the ports, have a tendency to be invisible.

The juxtaposition of successful industry and urban decay in the landscape of the UK is certainly not confined to the North. A town like Reading, with some of the fastest growth in the country (Microsoft, US Robotics, Digital, British Gas, Prudential Assurance), offers to a lesser degree exactly the same contrasts between corporate wealth and urban deprivation: the UK does not look anything like as wealthy as it really is. The dilapidated *appearance* of the visible landscape, especially the urban landscape, masks its prosperity. In November 1995, it was argued that in eighteen years of Conservative government the UK had slipped in a ranking of the world's most prosperous economies in terms of GDP per head, but it is equally likely that the position had remained unchanged, and in any case this was only a ranking amongst nations all of which had become increasingly wealthy. If the UK had slipped in this table, it had not slipped anything like as much as, say, Australia or Sweden, or even the Netherlands. The UK's GDP was then the fifth largest in the world after the US, Japan, Germany and France. What had changed was the distribution of wealth.

¶ page 194 The Barrow shipyard was completed in 1871 and acquired by Vickers in 1897. In 1977, it was nationalized as part of British Shipbuilders, and it became VSEL (Vickers Shipbuilding Engineering Ltd) in an employee-led privatization in 1986. In 1995, it was bought by GEC after an investigation by the Monopolies and Mergers Commission and a counter-bid from British Aerospace. GEC is a major defence exporter, controversially to Indonesia, supplying electronic systems for Hawks and to re-equip F5 fighters. In 1995, its chairman was Lord Prior, the former Cabinet minister. In March 1998, GEC-Marconi hired Jonathan Aitken as a consultant to advise on arms sales to the Middle East, but three weeks later, following Aitken's arrest and questioning, GEC said that his project was 'almost complete'.

¶ page 196 An audit of waste management at Sellafield and Drigg by HM Nuclear Installations Inspectorate and HM Inspectorate of Pollution was published in February 1996. It found material stored in steel drums in damp, unventilated earth-covered brick-and-concrete buildings. There was evidence of water penetration and corrosion; some drums had corroded so much that they had lost their contents. The nature of the contents was often not known. The buildings were originally built as temporary stores, as until 1983 much of the material was dumped at sea. Regular inspection was minimal, and in one building the audit team were required to wear all-over *Windscale* suits with air supply in case there was airborne contamination.

220

¶¶ page 196 The long-term future of high-level radioactive waste, presently stored above ground, was not part of Nirex's brief. This is an issue that has never been properly addressed by the nuclear industry itself, and probably never will be. The second report of the British Government Panel on Sustainable Development, published in January 1996, states: 'How to dispose of radioactive waste safely in perpetuity is one of the most intractable problems currently facing industrial countries.'

With permanent disposal unfeasible, the continuing operation of nuclear power plants leads to an accumulation of lethal waste. At present, the only practical course of action for radioactive waste is one of interim ground-level storage, so that both the problem and the knowledge of how to manage it are passed to future generations, who may or may not be able to devise more effective technological strategies.

A Conversation with Patrick Keiller

Patrick Wright: *Robinson in Space* came out in early 1997, but you had been working on it for several years before that. Where did it all begin?

Patrick Keiller: The first public screenings of *London* [the first *Robinson* film] were at the Berlin Film Festival in February 1994. I arrived in Berlin with two paragraphs outlining a sequel which was to be some kind of critique of English 'gentlemanly' capitalism. *London* was well received in Berlin, and I was offered a residency there the following year, so we structured the project to be made partly in the south of England and partly in Berlin, with visits to Prague and other places. It was supposed to be a comparison between the *look* of the south of England and that of landscapes where design and manufacturing had been and still were part of the culture.

PW: So you were going to use Middle Europe as a counterpoint?

PK: Yes – I'm interested in the link between subjectivities like that of Surrealism, which transform experience of what already exists, and the activities of designers, architects and manufacturers, who produce *new things*. *London* was a project which aimed to change experience of its subject, and so is *Robinson in Space*, but in *Robinson in Space* the subject is production – the production of new space and the production of artefacts. England is interesting because it is a society, a culture, which appears to be largely uninterested in producing its own artefacts, which is not the case in, say, Germany – not yet anyway – and was not the case here when I was a child.

PW: Can you explain how *Robinson in Space* relates to *London*?

PK: Well, *London* claims to be a document of the research of someone called Robinson, and its reception suggested another film in which Robinson researched something else, something that wasn't London. In *London*, Robinson predicts that he will lose his job, and in the synopsis I took to Berlin I wrote that, as a result of this, 'He leaves London, becoming an itinerant student of the English landscape, its economy and the sexuality of its inhabitants. He travels to the sites mentioned in the continual revelations about arms trading – little-known ports, run-down factories in back streets in the West Midlands. He reads Borges's *Garden of Forking Paths*. He wishes to become a spy, but is not sure whom to approach.'

Also, towards the end of *London* there is a line – 'The true identity of London is in its absence' – to which the viewer might reply: 'Absence of what?' London began and grew as a port city; its port activity is

223

now mostly absent, but it continues elsewhere. *Robinson in Space* was an attempt to locate some of the economic activity that no longer takes place in cities.

As well as the England–Berlin project there was another version, a 'Plan B' – in the end the version which appealed more to the BBC – which was to do a tour of England in the manner of Defoe, but in each case the motive was to explore a perception of the southern English economy – a lot of well-off people living in a suburban architecture, driving imported cars to John Lewis to buy consumer electronics and so on which have been made somewhere else and you don't know where it is . . . though of course it might be Wales, but we don't know that yet.

PW: But Wales is a kind of Japan. . .

PK: Yes . . . I already had an inkling that my perception of the UK's economy was completely out of date. It was an '80s perception.

PW: So you were investigating what, a few years previously, would have seemed a characteristically 'Thatcherite' reality.

PK: Yes. At about this time there was a piece in the *Financial Times* by James Morgan, who is or was the BBC World Service's economics correspondent. He began with a report in the *Spectator* of a meeting of a local Tory party association where 'when a man stood up to announce he would be standing as an anti-federalist, against a Tory candidate, in June's Euro-elections, the ovation from his fellow Conservatives verged on the hysterical'. Morgan identified this meeting as having taken place 'just outside Ewell, Surrey [the landscape that Robinson wished had been destroyed by H. G. Wells's Martians, or suspects of having been subjected to an *Invasion of the Body Snatchers*], in the function room of Ye Olde Cocke House Inne, which stands between the Wok-on-By Chinese restaurant and a kitchenware shop call Hôte Cuisine. There was a delicious meal (breaded scampi on a bed of lettuce 'garnished with all the trimmings'). Morgan went on to quote Fernando Vallespin, in *El Pais*, as identifying 'a connection which almost always exists between repressive societies and liberal states'. He continued: '. . . a liberal state has to impose artificial rules to replace the glue that exists in traditional systems. There rules are broken easily without society falling to bits. Britain is no more a traditional society than Ye Olde Cocke House Inne is a traditional inn.'

There is a certain English attitude which sees no inconsistency between driving a BMW and being anti-German. I wanted to explore the landscape which is the result of this, in the context of a widespread belief that the UK has lost most of its manufacturing industry, and that this is a matter for regret because somehow an identity has gone with it, and because manufacturing industry is good for the community. This was a set of beliefs one encountered especially amongst people of my generation, especially in the '80s. Coming from the North, with

224

very distant memories of the 1950s, I imagined I might have grown up in a town where railway locomotives were regularly carried through the middle of town on the way from workshops to the docks – though I'm sure I never saw this except in photographs. As far as one could gather, Thatcher hated manufacturing – it was to be got rid of. We were all to live on 'financial services', to make our livings selling life insurance to one another. Now, of course that doesn't work – it wouldn't work anywhere. 'Financial services' don't bring in enough export earnings, so there's nothing to pay for the BMWs. So there's a big question: If everything in the shops is imported, and everybody works in mostly non-exporting service industries, how is this sustainable? It doesn't look nice, but probably that doesn't matter – one gets used to it, it's all right, it's heterogeneous. England probably hasn't looked 'authentic' since the agricultural workforce was 'down-sized' in the nineteenth and early twentieth centuries. This is why we have so little indigenous cuisine and so on. In the end, one questions this kind of authenticity, but there remain the questions of how the UK pays for its imports, where they come from and how they get here.

PW: And in that same floating world, financial concentration was ensuring that all the high streets in the country were converging: the same shops and street furniture everywhere, so that the very idea of a distinct place was becoming abstract, 'heritage' as the twin of industrial dereliction.

PK: In 1993 I'd gone to live in Oxford. When we arrived, the greater part of the car factory in Cowley was being demolished. What was left was producing two Honda-based Rover models and a few Montegos for export. Then in January 1994, British Aerospace sold Rover (as it was by then called) to BMW, and developed the cleared site as a business park. It turned out that Bernd Pischetsrieder, the BMW chairman, was the great-nephew of Alec Issigonis.

PW: Issigonis being a great designer...

PK: Issigonis redesigned the car in the '60s, and offered BMC the possibility of being first in a world market.

PW: ...who comes out of Turkey and conceives the Morris Minor.

PK: Yes, during the war.

PW: And then he designs the Mini, and they throw it away.

PK: He designed the Morris Oxford (which survives in India as the Ambassador), the Morris Minor, the Mini and the 1100, which in the early '60s was the biggest-selling British car and was designed as a 'world car', fifteen years before the VW Golf. It's the same concept, but BMC threw away the initiative . . . either because they were provincial conservatives and wanted to go on selling Austin Cambridges to men in trilby hats, or because the car industry was a casualty of the UK's failure to join the EU in the '60s, which is a much more plausible explanation. Issigonis's space-economy concept worked best for medium-sized and small cars, which need big markets to be profitable. With big cars, the engineering tends to be more conservative – Mercedes and BMWs still have rear-wheel drive. Technological innovation didn't sell at the top end of the market, and without international sales the bottom end of the market didn't work. As a result of that – well, either that or innate conservatism – the company brought in people from Ford and other non-automotive concerns who tried to make a car to compete with the Ford Cortina. The result was the Morris Marina, which was a failure.

PW: Yes, and then the Metro. . .

PK: Then the Allegro, which was a botched development of the 1100, and then the Metro, Maestro and Montego.

PW: With the Metro, you had to get on your knees to put petrol in the tank; it was a depression car.

PK: There is a market for Montegos though. Interestingly, Blair. . .

PW: He pulled into Downing Street in one. . .

PK: In a Montego estate car. . .

PW: . . . with a hubcap missing.

PK: It's a cheap seven-seat estate car, a doctor's car.

PW: I thought it was a car for retired people.

PK: No, it's for people with four kids. It's cheaper than a Peugeot, it's cheaper than a Volvo – difficult to sell, I'm told, but where I live they're quite common. They're probably all right – robust cars. They sent them to Siberia. . .

PW: So *Robinson in Space* is about that rather shapeless, chaotic, constantly transforming reality that emerged in the Home Counties in the '80s.

PK: There were these questions: How does the UK pay for its imports? Does it still have a manufacturing sector that exports, and if so, what is it? Where do all the *visible* imported artefacts come from, and why don't we see them until they are in the shop window? When I was a child, I used to see truckloads of 'Prestcold' fridges on the road, but now none of this is visible until it arrives in the shops. How does it get there? Where does it come ashore? Is it at Felixstowe? At Southampton? Where are the UK's ports? Where are the spatial locations of import and export?

Robinson had moved to Reading, which is a very interesting place; there have been an unusually large number of television documentary series made about Reading. *The Family* was made in Reading, and the series about the Thames Valley Police. It also has a good art school, which has a respectability that Robinson might try to attach himself to.

PW: And it's also got that mixture you describe as characteristic
of present-day England: extreme dilapidation plus conspicuous
wealth, a telling combination.

PK: It's the fastest-growing region in the country. Berkshire has the
fastest-growing population.

PW: But how does wealth coincide with ruin, in this theory? In a
town like Reading – actually you pick this up throughout the film –
you've got dereliction and also this sense of emergent prosperity.

PK: I think there's a distinction between *new space* and *old space*. *New
space* is so-called *market-driven* space – somewhere like Thames Valley
Park in Reading: a business park. Microsoft have built a big site at
Thames Valley Park; you can see it from the train. There is a lot of
new space – a lot of distribution estates, a lot of leisure parks.

PW: It's an interesting disjunction. If you consider what towns
looked like under a more social-democratic dispensation, there was
always an idea, it was probably a pastoral myth most of the time,
but it was there nevertheless, that wealth generally improves the
neighbourhood. This was part of the planning mechanism, and it
was also what the advocates of gentrification assumed: that
middle-class incomers may make a killing on rising house values,
but the schools tend to get better and shops improve. But your
Robinson is going out into a world where the wine-bar and 'uplift'
scenario has failed, and where the idea of a link between new
wealth and general recovery or commonwealth seems to be busted
completely.

PK: Yes, perhaps, but I think there's another reason. Although there is
a lot of *new space*, and one tends to think of it as being modern, 70 per
cent of urban space is residential, and residential space is untouched
by any of this. Residential space is *old space* and getting older: in the
last twenty years, house-building has fallen steadily. The rate of
house-building is now very low – there is almost no public-sector
house-building, and houses are hardly ever replaced. Rich people's
houses are dilapidated too – dilapidation doesn't result only from
poverty – for a global economy, anything local is very difficult to
deal with, and you can't get much more local than a house. House
maintenance is a consumer's nightmare. The bits of the economy that
deal with the home simply don't work very well. The telephones
work; it's not the home itself that doesn't work, it's the physical fabric
of the house. The brickwork is crumbling, and this seems to be the
case for rich and poor alike, not equally perhaps, but unless one
spends an enormous amount of money it's very difficult to keep up
old space. But it seems to be equally impossible to replace it. This isn't
the same everywhere in the world – the Japanese economy produces
technologically sophisticated artefacts, and one of the artefacts it
produces is the industrialized house. House-replacement is quite
common in Japan, but here, because we don't produce many artefacts

or aren't very good at it or have to get other people to organize it for us, our housing is a mess. Looking back to the time of Engels, one wonders if this hasn't always been the case, as if house-building is somehow inimical to industrial capitalism. The best period for house-building in the UK was probably the time of the Arts and Crafts Movement, which grew out of an opposition to industrial capitalism. In Japan, Toyota got involved in house production only because there is a tradition that each generation of the Toyoda family has to initiate a new business, and Nissan had already decided to develop space-travel.

PW: So let's get back to this curious reality which emerged in the '80s: vast retail sheds along the bypass; ports that are invisible in the sense that nobody works there any more, and the dockers and stevedores have given way to containers. You show a lot of barriers, a lot of wire, a lot of security cameras, a lot of private or privatized institutions, even prisons – these are some of the distinctive features of the world that you are focusing on.

PK: Yes.

PW: Did you go out looking for that, or is it just as you got off the train or off the motorway, this is what you saw? There you are, like Robinson eating in supermarkets, staying in roadside motels – is this just how the film composed itself as you went along?

PK: I think it's mostly as we found it. Partly because we were travelling by road, we didn't make many pictures in cities. From the film's point of view, the most interesting city was probably Manchester – that was the only time we really made many pictures in a city. The subject was *new space*, and generally *new space* is found outside or on the edge of cities. The pictures are more or less what we found. In fact, we didn't find it for a long time; we spent quite a lot of time early on in the project wondering where the *new space* was – it wasn't visible enough. It did change: as we went along, it became more aggressive – the points on the fence got sharper; the difference between a prison and a supermarket became more difficult to discern; the atmosphere became more S&M. Again, I had a preconception about this, an idea that there is something up in the countryside, that the countryside is actually a rather forbidding place. The town seems more friendly, generally speaking.

PW: People still walk in the towns.

PK: They walk about . . . The countryside seems more scary. I don't know how real this is because I don't live in the countryside.

PW: I do, but I don't have a lot to do with it. I come to London to go for a walk.

PK: There's a film called *Night of the Eagle* made in 1961, with Peter Wyngarde as a lecturer at an educational institution in a country house with large eagles on its gate-posts. His colleagues are practising witchcraft, which (I think) leads to some chilling effect involving the eagles. I remember it whenever I drive past a pair of monumental gate-posts. There's a new Gothic genre in the present-day English countryside. . .

PW: We've talked about this strangely placeless contemporary surface of the landscape, but I want to ask you about history, about the past, because it seems to be a very strong presence in this film none the less, despite everything you're saying. You've got those white chalk figures in the green hillside – Cerne Abbas, Wilmington. You show these things almost as pauses, silent moments without words spoken over them, and you even turn off those ubiquitous birds you've scattered throughout the film. Does history as it is still written in the landscape provide some sort of perspective on the contemporary overlay? I mean, there's Robinson, looking for Rimbaud at the beginning, and digging up all sorts of cultural references as he goes. Is history just disconnected debris, or does Robinson find it still potent and challenging?

PK: He's always trying to reconstruct his culture, so he looks for things which will enable him or other people to do the same.

PW: So, he's a reconstructor in that sense?

PK: Yes. He comes to Oxford and picks out Robert Burton, because *The Anatomy of Melancholy* was an important source for Laurence Sterne, and because Sterne was an important source for the Russian Formalists, for Shklovsky – for modernism, for the cinema, for the twentieth century. There's also the Neolithic rock art at the end, topographical abstract art – very contemporary, very modern, very international.

PW: As I watched *Robinson in Space* I found myself thinking about being driven in cars as a child in the early '60s: particularly the A4 in Wiltshire, and almost certainly in a Morris Minor. I remember passing those great historic presences around Avebury, Silbury Hill, and the many barrows on the skyline in that area, and getting a very palpable sense from that landscape that life was once completely otherwise. Do you feel concerned that the potency of the historical landscape is reduced by the curiously placeless landscape of 'new space', with its wire, its estates and its giant retail sheds? Is that part of your concern in this film?

PK: I don't think it's diminished that much visually. I think it's threatened more in other ways. I read that skylark numbers have dropped by 50 per cent or so since not very long ago. When I was a child, I don't remember seeing skylarks very often, but I wasn't very mobile. They are on the decline – one doesn't distrust the figures – but somehow one is more aware of them, even though there are fewer birds. I certainly see more of them than I used to do, and not because I make films, just generally. And they are, I would imagine, more widely treasured than they were thirty years ago.

PK: Yes, and with all these things there's a kind of displacement. People don't seem to eat better just because the television is covered in cookery programmes. Domestic architecture doesn't get any better because the television is covered in make-over programmes. It seems to be a way of coping with it more than anything else. More people join Friends of the Earth, and yet car use goes on increasing – there is obviously a conflict. But going back to the sheds: they are very ephemeral, so in a way one doesn't worry too much about them. I don't see them as being inimical. One can imagine the future being a few sheds and a lot of dilapidated houses.

PW: Let's talk about Blackpool, because if Robinson's utopia comes true anywhere, you suggest that it is probably in Blackpool. You've got this wonderful line in the notes from the landscape designer who put so much of Blackpool together, and who apparently once observed that what stands between England and revolution is Blackpool.

PK: 'Blackpool stands between us and revolution' – which he appears not to have borrowed from Le Corbusier. I thought maybe he had read *Vers une architecture*, but he appears to have said it before the book was published in England, so it's unlikely. In Le Corbusier's book there is a chapter entitled 'Architecture or Revolution'.

PW: Is this the old argument about bread and circuses?

PK: No. Robinson says what he says in Blackpool because he is a surrealist and believes in the carnivalization of everyday life. Blackpool is probably the nearest you get to that . . .

PW: . . . in a mid-century form?

PK: Yes, or even earlier; the quotation is from the '20s. One can imagine that if Louis Aragon had come to England and someone had taken him to Blackpool, he might have been intrigued, and England wouldn't have been left off the Surrealist map of the world, although one doesn't know. Jennings went to Blackpool, and he doesn't seem to have had his life changed by it. But that's another story. The statement is based in *revolutionary subjectivity*; it's not about hitting the streets, it's about Blackpool as an alternative to hallucinogenic drugs. Which it seems to be: you can go to Blackpool and have a good day, but you can also go to Blackpool and have a bad day. Especially if you're a photographer and the sun doesn't come out, if you've got two days and one of them is no good. Maybe the next one is all right – that's what happened to us. The first day was dreadful. We had to wait until twilight to get a shot.

PW: Yes, it does look very gloomy in the photograph.

PK: The next day there was a gale. The wind was too strong for us to go up the tower. We waited with the men in red boiler suits who maintain it. It was a bit difficult, touch and go, but eventually we got up the tower and made these pictures of apocalyptic sunlight on the sea. Blackpool light is *radiation*, the sunlight up there: it's not just in the sea, it's everywhere. Absolutely terrifying, with the wind. The light is connected to the altered subjectivity which seems to go with . . . I don't know about a good day . . . with a successful visit to Blackpool. And Blackpool is modern – the Illuminations were borrowed from the Kaiser's birthday celebrations, and the tower is borrowed from the Eiffel Tower; the company which became Jaguar began in Blackpool, and they used to make aeroplanes there. The trams are very Middle European. You can imagine that it's the coast of Bohemia, if you're looking for the coast of Bohemia. . .

PW: With a certain amount of radioactivity added in there.

I'd like to talk to you about the way you close or end these films. In *Robinson* you've got a particular kind of camera use that is almost always static, and concerned with framing and putting lines around reality. You've avoided drama, so there are no people there, and in that sense no narrative strings to be tied up. I guess what happens is that Robinson goes into some sort of increased anxiety towards the end, and then he gets cancelled and the commission from this crazy London image consultancy which has told him to go off and investigate 'the problem of England' is withdrawn, and that's about it. Were you troubled by that, or is that the end the subject demands?

PK: Well, there are obvious ways of ending a narration. It's like the end of a life – consciousness stops. The story has a happy ending because it ends with a celebration of a place – the last shot is of the Tyne – but the narration ends before that. Robinson finds his revelations increasingly difficult to contain, and he is becoming increasingly involved with military subjects and espionage. . .

PW: And the state behind the state and all that stuff.

PK: He becomes obsessional about Buckminster Fuller. He thinks that there are buckminsterfullerenes in a piece of equipment in a Tornado, which is unlikely, but he climbs into Warton and tries to steal the piece of equipment. Somebody has a quiet word with the agency, and they drop him; his mobile phone's cut off, which is one reason why you see the image of the phonecard. They're back on the street; they've lost their privileges.

There is another happy ending, another side to Robinson's certainty which is perhaps less obvious. The project was exploratory, an attempt to find out what had happened to the manufacturing economy. When I was writing the narration, I had a clipping from 1994, an article by Bob Rowthorn entitled 'Brave new world of services exports is folly', which set out why the UK will never be able to sustain a trade balance by replacing manufactured exports with exports of services, because exports of services don't bring in enough to pay for imports. The UK's services exports had actually declined during the previous twenty-five years because of the decline of UK shipping and the rise of other service exporters. Manufactured items are still the major part of the UK's exports. 'Manufactured imports,' Rowthorn wrote, 'have not been financed by exports of services . . . but by the export of other manufactures, especially capital goods and intermediate products such as chemicals.' We set out to find the sites of these industries; the search culminated on Teesside, where we found the largest concentration of successful manufacturing industry (producing things like polypropylene chips to make car bumpers and crisp packets), as well as the highest rate of unemployment and some of the most striking urban decay. The realization which drives Robinson into his erratic behaviour is that the appearance of poverty that characterizes so much of modern Britain is not the result of the failure of the UK's capitalism, but of its success. The perception of economic failure and backwardness that worries aesthetes, especially people like me who grew up in the '60s, is based on a misunderstanding. The perception of decline that reduced our expectations of what the state can deliver – for education, the health service, state pensions and so on – is quite wrong. . .

PW: You phoned Rowthorn?

PK: I phoned him up while I was writing the script to confirm my perception a) of what he'd written and b) of what I'd found. He was talking about how the British economy is fairly well placed – we have agriculture, we have the City, oil, chemical exports; in those terms it's not really a problem. The question is whether it's very nice to live with. It works, on its own terms. The question I was asking, which is really one about the quality of life, is a completely separate question, a different question. To the question 'Does it work?' the answer is 'Yes, of course it works; otherwise we wouldn't have anything to eat.' Even so, a lot of people seem to have seen the film as a document of industrial decline. Most of the press, most of the arts press, usually said something about 'economic decline'; they haven't twigged.

PW: You're talking about *London* or *Robinson*?

PK: *Robinson*. As I read it, it's a document of transformation, a discovery of these out-of-the-way places where they make plasterboard. Why plasterboard?

PW: And in such huge quantities.

PK: For re-export.

PW: And little jetties, which are not known about, but which are used to ship weapons.

PK: All that –

PW: Semi-secrecy.

232

PK: And no one around. I always wondered where the present-day ports were, where imports arrived. One never goes to these places; they're all at the ends of roads, and if one does go to one of them they seem so insubstantial that one thinks they can't be that important. You'd never think that Immingham was a big port – there's nothing there.

PW: So does this film about England actually resolve into a film about a more general kind of capitalism?

PK: Recently, someone drew my attention to *The Pristine Culture of Capitalism* by Ellen Meiksins Wood, which was published in 1991. She asks more or less the same question: 'Is Britain, then, a peculiar capitalism or is it peculiarly capitalist?' She argues that the latter is true. What I find interesting about her book is that it is full of references to the things I have been photographing for years. For example:

'What American tourists today think of as the characteristically "European" charm of the major Continental cities – the cafés, the fountains, the craftsmanship, the particular uses of public space – owes much to the legacy of burgher-dom and urban patriciates . . . This kind of urban culture was overtaken very early in England by the growth of the national market centred in London . . . Today's urban landscape in Britain – the undistinguished modern architecture, the neglect of public services and amenities from the arts to transportation, the general seediness – is not an invention of Thatcherism alone but belongs to a longer pattern of capitalist development and the commodification of all social goods, just as the civic pride of Continental capitals owes as much to the traditions of burgher luxury and absolutist ostentation as to the values of modern urbanism and advanced welfare capitalism.'

She then quotes Hobsbawm, who wrote:

'The British roots of the "modernism" which led to the Bauhaus were, paradoxically, Gothic. In the smoky workshop of the world, a society of egoism and aesthetic vandals, where the small craftsmen so visible elsewhere in Europe could no longer be seen in the fog generated by the factories, the Middle Ages of peasants and artisans had long seemed a model of a society both socially and artistically more satisfactory.'

So, we're back to questions of design . . .

PW: And why not also the French town? I passed through Pau earlier this year, in the Pyrenees, and spent some time in this amazing public square called the Square of Resistance. It's got the war memorial, it's got fountains and it's got a church incorporated into it. That square embodied the monumental and the normally quiescent face of the state – a face which is absent from Robinson's England, except as punitive barbed wire, razor wire . . .

233

PK: Which brings us to sex. This is an issue which Ellen Wood doesn't deal with: 'Why are the English so keen on S&M?' Is S&M anything to do with England being 'peculiarly capitalist'? It isn't difficult to put together an idea that there is something sadistic about the implementation of the unregulated market – this seems to have been very strong in Thatcherism, for instance, inequality being very bad for people's health, and not only for poor people's health; Thatcher taking money from Philip Morris immediately after leaving office, that kind of thing.

PW: Your Robinson starts off with this brief from a research consultancy that has decided that the British brand is in need of remaking, that the traditional brand has to be thrown off. I guess you weren't surprised to see these ideas relaunched under New Labour, since you had already spotted a building opened by Mr Blair in his northern constituency, a very modest commercial building . . .

PK: For a company which had given money to the Tory party.

PW: Which company was that?

PK: Forte, before it was taken over by Gerry Robinson.

PW: But now that the Labour government has taken over the project of rebranding Britain and lifting the nation with logos, this is presumably the right time for Robinson to get sacked?

PK: Well, yes, he went early on. I think we're probably better off out of all that because I don't think it can work – there are far too many contradictions. The fancy-dress universities, for example, of which Blair is a product.

PW: He's started to look an awful lot like Prince Charles, especially in his mannerisms. Have you noticed?

PK: Does he? He comes across as this guy who played second guitar in a pop-group at Oxford, but when he was at Oxford, as far as I can gather, he spent a lot of time discussing theology with a middle-aged man from New Zealand in a bed-sit. Even so, it feels a different place from the one I lived in under the Tories. I used to feel . . . there was always a tension, a political tension . . . how can it go on? How can it last eighteen years? I was on a train about three days before the election, looking out of the window thinking, 'These people aren't going to vote Labour.' I thought I could hear people bottling out – 'Oh, I'm not sure, I don't think I'm going to change my vote after all.' But it was a complete fantasy. They won, beyond anyone's expectations.

PW: Including their own, which is perhaps why they started out so tentatively.

PK: I still haven't recovered from that.

PW: You mean as a critical film-maker?

PK: Immediately – never mind the politics – suddenly there was this mainstream in the middle of British culture.

PW: Again.

PK: Yes, again, and it was, 'Oh – is *that* what's happened?'

PW: So how have you responded? I mean, I'm sure you didn't get phoned by the new Culture Minister?

PK: No – I got phoned, but not by them. I had decided to make a film about housing. Sitting on the bus going up and down the A40, I developed this idea about houses. When we were making *Robinson*, I was thinking, 'Why aren't we doing any pictures of houses?' It was because there wasn't really anything of interest; even new houses were not part of *new space*. I used to sit in supermarket cafés gazing at houses beyond the carpark and wondering why the house seemed to be immune to the kind of computer-driven modernization that had enabled supermarkets all over England to offer an approximation of Mediterranean food that was once available only in Soho. There were cheap international phone calls, banking by telephone, sending e-mails from the kitchen sink, and a lot of other more or less electronic developments in domestic life, but in twenty years the physical fabric of the dwelling had hardly changed at all. Supermarkets were offering mortgages, but generally the private sector seemed unable to modernize house-building, at least in the UK. No one was interested in housing under Thatcher because all we ever thought about was leaving the country [*laughs*], but if Labour were going to get in, maybe this would change . . .

Acknowledgements

This book incorporates material from the film of the same name, which was developed with the assistance of its producer, Keith Griffiths, and commissioned by Tessa Ross and Roger Hyams for the BBC. Robinson was previously the protagonist of the film *London*.

Robinson in Space was photographed by Jason Hocking and myself between March and November 1995, with Jacqui Timberlake as production manager, assisted by Michaela Settle.

The images included in the film were selected by myself and Julie Norris, and edited by Larry Sider. I then wrote the story, aided by researchers Fiona Lloyd-Davies and Jason Hocking. The film's narrator was Paul Scofield.

The 221 images included here were selected from the film by myself and Julie Norris. I have made a few amendments to the original narrative and added marginal annotations and an appendix. The conversation with Patrick Wright took place in September 1998.

I would like to thank all of these people and everyone else who worked on the film, and all those who contributed to the project in many other ways.

P. K.
October 1998